W9-BGI-557

WAY *of*
Tibetan Buddhism

WAY *of*
Tibetan Buddhism

Lama Jampa Thaye

Thorsons

Thorsons
An Imprint of HarperCollins*Publishers*
77–85 Fulham Palace Road
Hammersmith, London W6 8JB

The Thorsons website address is: www.thorsons.com

Published by Thorsons 2001

1 3 5 7 9 10 8 6 4 2

© Lama Jampa Thaye 2001

Lama Jampa Thaye asserts the moral right to be
identified as the author of this work

A catalogue record for this book
is available from the British Library

ISBN 0 7225 4017 5

Printed and bound in Great Britain by
Martins The Printers Limited, Berwick upon Tweed

All rights reserved. No part of this publication may be
reproduced, stored in a retrieval system, or transmitted,
in any form or by any means, electronic, mechanical,
photocopying, recording or otherwise, without the prior
permission of the publishers.

Contents

To H.H. Sakya Trizin and
Karma Thinley Rinpoche

Acknowledgements

Adrian O'Sullivan made a major contribution to this book as did Rana Lister who drew the illustrations. My thanks to them and to Geoffrey Ashmore for their work. Finally, I would like to thank my wife Albena for all her help.

Foreword

༄༅། །ཕན་བདེའི་འབྱུང་གནས་དམ་པའི་ཆོས་ཉམས་སུ་ལེན་པ་

ལ། ཐོག་མར་ཆོས་ཀྱི་དོན་མ་ནོར་བ་ཤེས་པ་གལ་ཆེ་བས། དཔལ་འདིར་

གཞན་དང་རྒྱུ་མ་བྱ་མ་རྤ་མཐའ་ཡས་ནས་བརྒྱུམས་མཛད་པའི་རྩོལ

བསྟུན་དང་ཞིང་རྒྱས་ཆུལ། ཤེས་པ་གསུ་མ་ཀྱི་རྒྱ་མ་བཞག་ཆོགས་ལེགས

པར་བཞད་པ་འདིས། རང་ཆོས་ལ་དད་པས་སྨོན་འདོད་པ་རྣམས་ལ་ཕན་པ་རྒྱ

ཆེན་པོ་འབྱུང་བར་དེས་པས། ཐམས་ཅད་ཀྱིས་ཆོས་བསམ་གཏེར་ཟབ་མཛད

ནས། གཏན་བདེའི་དཔལ་ལ་སྤྱོད་པའི་སྨོན་ལམ་འདེ། ཅེས་པའང་།

ཕྱགས་འབྱུག་ལོ་དང་ ཕྱི་ལོ 2000 ཟླ་ན 4 ཆོས 25 དགེ་བར་དཔལ

ལེགས་བཞད་ཀྱིར་དུ། གཙུ་ཕྲེན་ལས་བཞི་མིང་པས་བྲེས་པ་དཔོ།

In order to practise Buddhism, the source of goodness and happiness, it is very important to have a correct understanding of its meaning. Therefore, in this book the Lord of Scholars, Lama Jampa Thaye, has explained both how the Buddha's teaching spread and how we are to practise the three vehicles.

I pray that all who study, reflect and meditate upon it will come to enjoy unchanging happiness.

The Fourth Karma Thinley

Written in the Iron Dragon Year, the 25th of April, 2000 at Legshe Ling, Bodhanath, Nepal.

Introduction

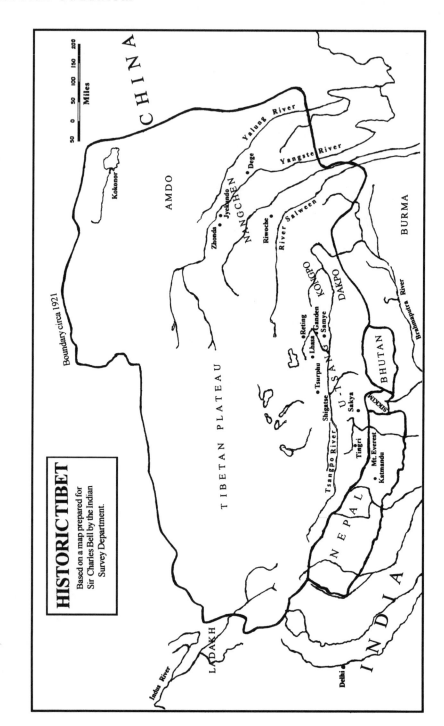

There is a story told about a poor man who lived a life of the utmost misery. All his life was spent in a pursuit of wealth. He journeyed everywhere in his search, until finally he expired alone in the small hut where he had been born. However, all the time unbeknownst to him an unimaginable pile of treasure had lain concealed beneath the floor.

Buddha has told us that each of us is that person. We look in every place for happiness. Some of us search for it in physical pleasure, some in power and some in religion. Yet it has always been within reach, for it is mind itself 'the king of all creators' which is the source of true joy, wisdom and compassion. It is this discovery that constitutes 'enlightenment', 'nirvana' or 'buddhahood'.

Nowadays everything seems broken; many spiritual traditions appear to have lost their effectiveness. Yet Buddha's teaching, especially as preserved in the Tibetan tradition of Buddhism, can speak to all of us directly whether we are young or old, rich or poor, male or female.

This book is designed as an introduction to this age-old yet startlingly contemporary tradition. It is written from the inside of the tradition but is aimed at a modern Western audience. It does not compromise the truth and beauty of Tibetan Buddhism but is structured so as to be accessible.

It is not a do-it-yourself book. There are no secret mantras or mandalas revealed. Such things must be received in the appropriate context from one's master when one is ready. However, for those who wish to see into the heart of Tibetan Buddhism this book offers the window.

ONE

THE ORIGINS OF
Tibetan Buddhism

The Origins of Tibetan Buddhism

Tibetan Buddhism is one of the last great religious traditions still alive in the world today. It is a tradition that at one time dominated much of central and northern Asia and now, remarkably, finds itself in the modern Western world. Despite all the vicissitudes of the centuries, its vitality and power are undiminished. It is a tradition that speaks directly to us as a science of mind and perhaps as a basis of a new civilization, a civilization based on the timeless qualities of wisdom and compassion.

What do we mean when we talk of Tibetan Buddhism? The very first thing that we should acknowledge is that 'Tibetan Buddhism' is really a term invented by Westerners. In Tibet, it is the *dharma*, meaning 'the truth'. That truth was announced some 2,500 years ago in India by the extraordinary figure we call the Buddha. However, for us in the modern world the term 'Tibetan Buddhism' can serve as a convenient designation for the particular type of Buddhism that has been practised in Tibet and in the surrounding areas such as Mongolia, Bhutan, Ladakh, Sikkim, parts of Nepal and even parts of Siberia.

It is important that we begin first with some study of the history of this spiritual tradition, because one of the most characteristic features of Tibetan Buddhism is its stress on the notion of *lineage*. This means the sequence of transmission of the teachings from one generation of practitioners to the next. For these teachings to be spiritually efficacious, for them to have the capacity to transform us, they must not have degenerated into mere words or slogans. They must be endowed with the power to awaken insight into the true nature of mind, as they were when first given by Buddha. Only the unbroken transmission from teacher to disciple can guarantee this continuation of power, because only those who have mastered the teachings are able to transmit them. That is why in order for us to have confidence that a tradition and a teaching can work, particularly for us as modern Westerners, we need first of all to ask, 'From where does this teaching come and who transmitted it?'

Shakyamuni, the Buddha of our present age

These are questions that will be answered in this first chapter where we will outline the spread of Buddhism from its beginnings in India up to its complete transmission to Tibet many years later. We will take up the story again in chapter 4, in which we discuss the schools of Tibetan Buddhism. These chapters on history will inevitably be rich in names. These are the names of the teachings that comprise the spiritual repository of Buddhism and the great men and women who preserved and transmitted it. Whilst at first these may appear unusual, as the names crop up in one place or other in this book we will begin to become familiar enough with them.

Buddhism in India

The Life of the Buddha

Buddha was born in the fifth or sixth century bc in Lumbini, a place now located within the modern-day kingdom of Nepal but, at the time, part of the general area that we might call north-eastern India. His birth is understood by his followers as the culmination of many lifetimes spent striving towards enlightenment, inspired by the resolution formed in his mind to bring limitless benefit to all beings. It is one of the most important principles of Buddhism that only through fulfilling such a resolution is enlightenment accomplished. Tibetans believe that the historical Buddha was merely one of countless buddhas who have appeared in the past and who will appear in the future. Indeed, the principle ideal of Tibetan Buddhism is that we should all seek to become buddhas, beings endowed with the unrestricted ability to help others.

The story of Buddha's early years is well-known. The first 29 years of his life were spent in the comparative luxury of his father's court, a luxury that shielded him from the brutal realities of life. Finally, his spiritual drive compelled him to look outside the gilded cage of his existence. He broke away from his royal entourage on various occasions to explore the streets of India, where he was confronted for the first time by the sufferings of old age, sickness and death. These experiences caused him to abandon his indulgent lifestyle in search of something more meaningful. Six years of hard spiritual toil followed in which he encountered diverse gurus who initiated him into the different currents of spiritual practice that were spreading rapidly throughout northern India at the time. Yet none of these teachers was able to guide him to the decisive understanding he sought concerning the origin of suffering itself, the suffering to which all beings are chained.

Finally, in his 35th year, Buddha gained the knowledge that he sought. At the place known as Bodhgaya he entered into a meditation from which he had vowed not to arise until enlightenment was accomplished. Looking into the very depths of his being, he saw that the cause of suffering is ultimately our attachment to self. Clinging to the existence of a self is actually the most fundamental of delusions, because the self is nothing other than a mistaken fiction that sets us apart from the rest of reality. Stripping out the last vestiges of his attachment to this self, Buddha became awakened. The very name 'Buddha' actually means 'Awakened One'. With this awakening the full uncovering of his innate qualities of compassion and wisdom took place. When Buddha later came to teach others the understanding he had achieved, he would insist that all of us possess the very same qualities. It is these, rather than selfishness and its associated prejudices, that constitute our genuine nature, which he called 'buddha nature'. The egocentric impulses we experience are accretions we have picked up over countless lifetimes. Our fundamental state is the awakened insight and compassion that

Buddha returned to on that night some 2,500 years ago in Bodhgaya.

Buddha appears at first to have been uncertain as to whether his realization could be communicated to others. Later, having gained confidence in the possibility that others too could see what he had seen, he accepted as his first disciples former colleagues from the years of asceticism and austerity that had preceded his enlightenment. Thus, at Varanasi some weeks after the enlightenment, Buddha spoke of his insight into the nature of the world. He expressed this in the famous teaching known as 'The Four Noble Truths', which are:

1   *the truth of suffering;*
2   *the truth of the cause of suffering –*
     attachment to self;
3   *the truth of the cessation of suffering –*
     nirvana;
4   *the truth of the path to the cessation of*
     suffering – 'The Noble Eightfold Path'.

This eightfold path comprises right view, right intention, right action, right speech, right livelihood, right effort, right mindfulness and right concentration.

These and other fundamental teachings given by Buddha attracted all those who wished to find a way to deliverance from suffering. There were, however, some amongst his disciples whose understanding of the teachings was more penetrating. For such disciples, the profound significance of the Buddha's message was that each of us should strive to become awakened not only in order to become free from suffering oneself, but above all to help others achieve liberation. For these disciples it is said, Buddha revealed the *mahayana*, or 'Great Vehicle', a term significant in contrast to the focus of his ordinary teachings, the *hinayana* or 'Lesser Vehicle', given for those whose focus was principally upon their own liberation. We can see, therefore, two major threads in Buddha's teachings, designated by the two terms, hinayana and mahayana. The teachings that comprise the mahayana are extraordinarily profound and vast. In the mahayana Buddha taught that the true nature of reality lies beyond all conceptual notions and is thus best characterized as emptiness, and that the supreme path is that of the *bodhisattva*, one who works for enlightenment impelled by his compassionate resolve to achieve the welfare of others.

Within the mahayana itself we can find a further set of teachings delivered by Buddha. These are the teachings known as the *tantras*, whence comes the doctrine known as *vajrayana*. Buddha communicated these skillful teachings only to particularly suitable students and as with some of the mahayana teachings he appears to have given his teachings by manifesting in a divine form rather than his own ordinary human body. It is for this reason that some sutras and tantras may even have been revealed by Buddha after his physical death. In the course of revealing such teachings Buddha would enjoin upon the audience, whether an individual or a group, the need for care and a degree of secrecy in the preservation of the tantras. The first recipient of these teachings was King Indrabhuti, who had asked Buddha for a form of spiritual practice that could be carried out successfully in the midst of ordinary life. Acceding to his request, Buddha bestowed the first tantra, known as Guhyasamaja upon him.

Buddha's human life ended at the age of 80 in the tiny village of Kusinagara in northern India. There, attended by close disciples, Buddha gave his last teaching; a demonstration of the inevitability of change and decay, a demonstration afforded by his very death. Thus, the Enlightened One passed away from earthly existence.

The Growth of Buddhism in India

Following the Buddha's death his disciples collected together all his instructions. The teachings of the hinayana were collected by 500 of his disciples and arranged into three groups or 'baskets'. These were the abhidharma (philosophy), the vinaya (monastic conduct) and the sutras (discourses of the Buddha). The teachings of the mahayana were collected by various bodhisattvas and committed, like the teachings of hinayana, to collective memory and then eventually to writing. Finally, the most secret of Buddha's teachings, the tantras, were also collected, largely through the direction of the bodhisattva Vajrapani. They also were committed to memory and finally, some several centuries later, put into writing.

In parallel to this solidification of the Buddha's teaching Buddhist communities sprang up throughout India. These comprised lay people, who practised as ordinary householders, and the monastic community, who renounced family and social status in order to engage in a life of celibacy and poverty. Thus monks and nuns followed the discipline set by Buddha in the 'vinaya', the works of monastic discipline. In the first two centuries, the major emphasis in the Buddhist community was upon the hinayana teachings, prized for their simplicity, clarity and nobility.

The Rise of Mahayana

Gradually, however, the mahayana teachings came to the fore. In the spread of mahayana many great masters figured that the two most outstanding were Nagarjuna and Asanga, dubbed the 'two great charioteers'. Nagarjuna, Asanga and their followers contributed to the systematization of the awesomely diverse teachings left behind by the Buddha. In their literary compositions they expanded, defended and codified the teachings so that their works became like a key to the treasure chest of dharma. From their teachings come the two great philosophical schools of mahayana; *madhyamaka* or 'Middle Way' and *chittamatra* or 'Mind Only'.

One might wonder if such fission was indicative of some kind of weakness in Buddhism. Actually, the contrary is true, since different methods of presenting the teachings afford a rich variety of ways for people to accomplish realization. As there are so many kinds of practitioners and as the dharma is extremely profound, it would be rather limiting if Buddhism comprised only a single explanation of the path to realization.

The Vajrayana

The vajrayana, the teaching of the tantras, was transmitted for many generations in secret and it was not until the medieval period that it came to any kind of prominence. From the eighth century AD onwards outstanding masters such as Saraha, Naropa and Virupa contributed to the revitalization of dharma through expounding and practising the tantric teachings. Such figures are known as the *siddhas*, 'the perfected ones'. They were yogins who displayed their transcendence of all dualistic preconceptions and fixations through their enlightened and sometimes shocking behaviour.

Thus, by the time Buddhism came to an end in India as a religious and social institution in the 13th century AD, three waves of teachings had successively flourished; the hinayana, the mahayana and the vajrayana. In the next section of this chapter, we shall see how

9

this flowering of spiritual genius was transplanted to Tibet, a country of snowy peaks and endless uplands which gave rise to perhaps the most astounding spiritual tradition that the world has ever seen.

The Transmission of Buddhism in Tibet

The Early Diffusion

The early diffusion of Buddhism in Tibet commenced during the reign of King Songtsen Gampo (AD 609–49), and came to a climax in the time of his great grandson, Trison Detsen (AD 756–97), who ruled in the second half of the eighth century. Trison Detsen presided over Tibet at the time of its greatest territorial expansion, and yet political considerations appeared to have been subordinated to his vision of making Tibet a Buddhist country. He went a step further than his predecessor when he decided that the successful establishment of Buddhism in Tibet was dependent on the development of monasticism. In India, the monasteries had been the nerve centres of Buddhism where the practices of contemplation and study could be carried out unhindered.

In AD 770 Trison Detsen invited the philosopher and abbot Shantarakshita from India. His request to Shantarakshita was that he should consecrate the first Buddhist monastery in Tibet and ordain the first Buddhist monks. The monastery was to be constructed some 35 miles south-west of Lhasa and known as Samye Ling. Shantarakshita set to work on the construction of the temple and the monastic complex but opposition arose from two sources. At the mundane level, Trison Detsen's plans for Buddhism were challenged by a number of significant aristocratic families in central Tibet who resented both the power of the king and the coming of an alien religion to Tibet. At a more subtle level the local spiritual forces of Tibet also attempted to hinder the construction. It is said that whatever work the builders completed during the day would be undone at night by the ill-disposed *nagas*, snake-like spirits. Shantarakshita was eventually forced to admit to the king his inability to overcome these obstacles, realizing that only someone endowed with the powers bestowed by vajrayana would be equal to the task of overcoming such opposition. So it was that Shantarakshita suggested to the king that a vajrayana master be invited from India to overcome these difficulties. This master was to be no less than the greatest of all contemporary masters of the vajrayana, Padmasambhava, the Lotus Born one from the land of Oddiyana, a place probably to be identified with the modern-day border area of Afghanistan and Pakistan.

The Coming of Padmasambhava

Padmasambhava has been regarded by many Tibetan Buddhists as a second Buddha. His life history itself is a portrait of the qualities of enlightenment in action, beginning with his magical appearance as an eight-year old boy on a lotus flower in the middle of Lake Dhanakosha in Oddiyana, and continuing through his many years of study, meditation and miraculous activity in the lands of India, Nepal and Bhutan. These were years in which he acquired the full range of teachings of the hinayana, mahayana and vajrayana from a variety of masters. In short, as Shantarakshita told the king, there was nobody more qualified to ensure the successful transplantation of Buddhism to Tibet than Padmasambhava.

Trison Detsen's ministers and messengers found Padmasambhava in meditation-retreat in Nepal where he had removed many obstacles facing the local people. At their entreaties the master accepted the King's invitation and began to make his way slowly to central Tibet. At each step of the way the native Tibetan deities rose up against him, only to find themselves overcome by the force of his magical power. Each of these deities submitted to Padmasambhava and offered him their very life-force. Accepting their submission he bound them on oath to become guardians of Buddhism in Tibet.

Arriving at Samye, Padmasambhava was greeted by Trison Detsen and his court. At first the king's pride made him reluctant to make the customary prostrations with which one should honour one's tantric master. However, when Trison Detsen's robes burst into flames at the glance of Padmasambhava, he swiftly repaired his omission. Once assured of the king's devotion, Padmasambhava finally set to work in pacifying the most troublesome of spirits, the ones who opposed the construction of Samye Ling itself. This was quickly achieved through Padmasambhava's power and the temple construction could at last be completed. Shantarakshita himself ordained the first Tibetan monks, a group of seven young men drawn from the aristocratic clans who would be known as the 'seven probationer monks'.

While Shantarakshita and his disciples subsequently began the work of translating the sutras and their commentaries, Padmasambhava moved on to the second phase of his work in Tibet, the bestowal of the vajrayana teachings upon a group of 25 disciples. This group included the king, various great scholars such as Vairochana, and perhaps most importantly of all, the young Tibetan woman who would become both the Guru's closest disciple and his consort, Yeshe Tsogyal of the Kharchen family. On these disciples, Padmasambhava, now also known as *Guru Rinpoche*, the 'Precious Guru', bestowed his most powerful and secret teachings, those of the 'inner' tantras, techniques that permit the rapid transformation of an individual into a fully enlightened buddha. They comprise three sets of practices known as maha-yoga, anu-yoga and ati-yoga. Padmasambhava first initiated each of the 25 disciples into one of the 'eight major deities' of maha-yoga. Yeshe Tsogyal herself became an adept of the deity Vajrakilaya. Accompanying these initiations, the Guru also gave some instructions on anu-yoga and, most importantly of all, ati-yoga, the climax of all the teachings. Ati-yoga introduces us directly to the primordial state of enlightenment. This was the greatest of all the spiritual jewels that Padmasambhava had brought with him from India.

Padmasambhava was not alone in this work of seeding Tibet with vajrayana teachings. One of the other major figures involved during this period was the Indian yogin Vimalamitra who, like the Precious Guru, was an exponent of ati-yoga.

Thus, the conversion of the local Tibetan demons and gods and the transmission of the tantric teachings to his disciples were the first two of the major acts of Padmasambhava in Tibet. The third and final major deed was his concealment of a multiplicity of teachings intended for the benefit of future generations of dharma practitioners. These teachings, subsequently known as *ter-ma*, 'treasures', comprised spiritual instructions which were to be discovered and decoded in later centuries by masters whose minds had been blessed by Padmasambhava himself. These masters were later known as *tertons*, 'treasure-revealers'. The preservation of Padmasambhava's teachings as concealed treasures would be of incalculable benefit for Buddhism at a later time in Tibet. **13**

Eventually Padmasambhava took leave of his Tibetan disciples to work for beings in other lands. However, he assured his followers that he would never truly be apart from them since his compassion was 'beyond near and far'. He told them in particular that on the sacred tenth day of each month he would come riding on the rays of the sun from the Palace of Lotus Light to bless his faithful disciples. Such was Padmasambhava's promise – a promise that has remained unbroken down to the present day.

The Council of Lhasa

The last significant act of Trison Detsen's reign took place in 792. Shantarakshita had by that time passed away and the Precious Guru Padmasambhava had also departed from Tibet, leaving behind the treasures as his bequest for future generations. It was at this time that a great debate took place in Lhasa between those who followed the teachings that had come from India with Shantarakshita and Padmasambhava, and those who followed various Chinese Buddhist teachers who had also been active in the country. The debate revolved around the issue of how one should practise the mahayana. The Indian side proposed the view that one should follow a gradual approach to enlightenment, in which one acquires enlightened qualities in progressive stages. The Chinese masters taught that enlightenment was immediately accessible merely through the cessation of conceptual thought. The outcome of the debate was a decisive victory for the Indian party, led by Kamalashila, a disciple of Shantarakshita. As a result of this, Trison Detsen ordered that only the Buddhist teachings from India would be followed in Tibet. Thus, from then on, the guarantee of a teaching's orthodoxy in Tibet was its Indian origin.

If Songtsen Gampo and Trison Detsen were the first two great dharma kings of Tibet, the third one was the monarch known as

Ralpachen (806–41). He continued the policy of his predecessors and monasteries multiplied in number and influence. Ralpachen was succeeded by his half-brother Langdarma ('the Ox-headed One'). He had developed a violent antipathy towards the Buddhist teachings and ordered the closure of all monasteries, which by then dotted central Tibet. His actions struck a devastating blow to monastic study and practice, although he was unable to disrupt the lay tantric yogins who were active in the preservation of Padmasambhava's teachings. Finally, Langdarma was assassinated by the monk Palgyi Dorje who, foreseeing not just the damage that the king's actions would cause to Buddhism but also the suffering the king himself would reap from his negative actions, liberated him from his earthly existence. Despite this however, monasticism could not be revived and Tibet itself plunged into a long period of instability in which there was no central monarchy. This dark period for Tibet and the dharma lasted for some 150 or more years.

The Later Diffusion

Buddhism did not completely disappear from the Tibetan scene following the disastrous policies of Langdarma but monastic and scholarly forms were very severely damaged. Only the lineages of lay vajrayana practitioners were unbroken. By the eleventh century however, a significant number of people, including influential rulers from the province of Ngari in western Tibet, desired to see the re-establishment of the full range of Buddhist teachings and practices. They particularly wished to see the return of the scholarship and moral purity of monastic Buddhism. Their determination in this respect was undoubtedly fuelled by certain abuses that were taking place in areas of ritual and meditation practice by those who falsely claimed the sanction of vajrayana.

The first step taken by the royal family of Ngari to remedy the disorder in Buddhism was to sponsor the training of young Tibetan scholars in India. During that time such subsequently influential translators as Rinchen Zangpo and Drokmi were sent to India, beginning a new period of translation for the dharma teachings. This second period of transmission of Buddhism in Tibet is often called 'the period of the new translations'. Western Tibet was the home of this burgeoning renaissance of Buddhism.

Atisha

However significant the activity of these individuals was for the revitalization of Buddhism in Tibet, it was the Indian master known as Atisha Dipankara Shrijnana (979–1053) who undoubtedly made the greatest contribution. Atisha was invited by the royal family of Ngari in 1040 to render Buddhism in Tibet whole once more. He was to undo the damage inflicted during the dark period by setting out an authoritative model of the spiritual path, in which each facet of Buddha's teachings could be understood in its proper place and context. In short, Atisha was to set out a graduated path to enlightenment.

Atisha, master of the second transmission of Buddhism to Tibet

What made Atisha so uniquely fitted for this task? He had unparalleled expertise in the teachings of the sutras and tantras. Born in Bengal to a princely family, he had begun his Buddhist career as a disciple of various tantric masters and so was fully versed in vajrayana. However, at the age of 30, following a vision of the Buddha himself, he ordained as a monk and subsequently spent several years studying all the extant schools of Buddhism in India. He acquired mastery over all the philosophical teachings preserved in these schools but found that even this extensive training was not sufficient. He subsequently travelled to Suvarnadvipa (the present-day Sumatra) to receive a series of teachings on the generation of compassion from a teacher called Dharmakirti. These were the teachings of bodhichitta, the heart of the mahayana. As a result of his many years spent in such diligent study and practice, Atisha had become a true embodiment of the qualities of insight and gentleness. He is often identified with Manjushri, the bodhisattva of wisdom, who symbolized such qualities. Thus in Tibet it was not merely his authoritative text 'The Lamp of the Path to Enlightenment' which commanded the respect of his audiences but also the sheer force and goodness of his personality. When Atisha passed away in 1053 in Nyetang, north of Lhasa, he left behind his most precious gift to the Tibetan people; the gift of the *lam-rim* teachings, the 'graduated path' to enlightenment. This period marked the arrival of the second great wave of Buddhism in Tibet and the development of the major schools and thus is the time in which we can first distinguish between the old and the new transmission periods.

It is easy to see just how great the inheritance of the Tibetans was from the Buddhists of India. They received every form of Buddhist teaching, from the simplicity and austerity of monasticism through to the great philosophical insights of mahayana, and finally the esoteric techniques of the vajrayana. These three kinds of teachings, animated by the heartbeat of compassion, were jewels from the very mind of the Buddha, flawlessly preserved in India and now the inheritance of the Tibetans. Thus, it was inevitable that Tibetan men and women would in turn come to realize the ultimate fruits of spiritual practice. As we shall see in subsequent chapters, the land of Tibet spawned a host of wondrous masters.

Finally, we should note that the process of transmission from India to Tibet took several hundred years to complete and during that time there were numerous interruptions and disruptions that had to be overcome. That they were indeed overcome is a testimony to the determination of the Tibetan people. They persevered patiently in the task of receiving the teachings. Having received them, they preserved them without the corruption of alterations which, although more suitable to their prejudices or predilections, would rob the teachings of their power.

TWO

THE COMMON
Foundations

Buddha seems to have been a supremely skilful teacher who recognized that men and women came to him from an enormous variety of backgrounds, with different needs, different preconceptions and different strengths and weaknesses. He provided teachings and instructions to suit each one of them, showing the best way in which they could discover the qualities of enlightenment. As a result, following his 45 years of teaching, Buddhism was endowed with an extensive treasury of spiritual techniques. Nowhere has this treasury been preserved more faithfully than in Tibetan Buddhism.

Usually when Tibetans categorize the repertoire of teachings and instructions that they inherited from India, they do so in terms of two 'vehicles', which we have already referred to, namely the hinayana (lesser vehicle) and mahayana (great vehicle). Whilst this is a very useful means of categorization, we should avoid the mistake of imagining that because the mahayana is the superior of the two, we can simply eschew the practices of the hinayana. The Tibetans have never taken such an approach. Instead, they understand that the teachings of the so-called 'lesser vehicle' serve as the first step towards more advanced practices. So in this chapter we will look at those teachings which represent the common foundations of both hinayana and mahayana.

The two teachings upon which we will concentrate here are known as 'taking refuge' and *the Four Seals*. In Tibetan Buddhism it is said that one becomes a Buddhist of **conviction** by taking refuge in the Three Jewels and a Buddhist of **understanding** when one has understood the truth of the teachings embodied in the Four Seals, the fundamental axioms of existence propounded by Buddha. Let us consider these two teachings in turn so that we can come to understand their significance.

Taking Refuge

There is something almost ironic in the fact that becoming a Buddhist is called 'taking refuge', since we could say that throughout our life we have been taking refuge in all types of objects in order to acquire security, protection and happiness. Yet, when we honestly investigate whether any of these objects have brought us any real benefits, we must conclude that they have not.

For instance, if we take refuge in or rely on our body and its capacity for pleasure, we will discover that the body is impermanent and subject to all kinds of problems. How can such a thing provide a lasting happiness or security? If we take refuge in our relationships, we will discover that they never quite provide the contentment and wholeness that we so desperately crave. Even when there is a genuine exchange of affection and commitment there is the inevitability of parting. If we take refuge in philosophy or in politics, we are seeking happiness in mere intellectual creations. They cannot prove to be a source of protection from the many kinds of suffering we have encountered and will continue to encounter in this world. If we follow a religious tradition that involves pinning our hopes on some kind of powerful being who we believe will protect us, we will ultimately be left defenceless. Even where such powerful spirits exist they cannot provide protection from the cycle of birth and death any more than they can protect themselves from it. In other cases, what we might think of as a god does not exist even in a conventional sense and is merely the projection of human longings.

In short, there is nothing to which we can go for genuine refuge except that which is totally dependable. There are three sources of refuge, the so called 'Three Jewels' – the Buddha, the dharma (his teachings) and the sangha (his followers).

1. The Buddha

The Buddha is a suitable source of refuge because he discovered the true nature of reality and so is wholly dependable as a guide. By taking refuge in him, we are protected by the force of the truth of enlightenment and thus, although he is no longer physically present in the world, the blessings of his inspiration are. Although he is no longer physically present in the world, his blessings continue to be all-pervasive.

Buddha made it clear that he was not the first person in history to discover the nature of reality. Since the emptiness that actually characterizes all phenomena is one and the same throughout all time, there must have been countless individuals who had discovered it before him, just as one could imagine them doing so now in other world systems. Buddha merely uncovered the true nature of things at a time when it had been obscured. Buddha was thus a rediscoverer of a timeless truth. Buddha is also an exemplification of what we can be. To rely on him is to see our own true nature reflected in him. We therefore take refuge in the Buddha as our teacher and exemplar, relying on him as the guiding principle in our life and in the unfolding of our buddha nature.

2. The Dharma

The dharma, the teaching of Buddha, is a suitable source of refuge because it will lead us to enlightenment. By practising the instructions and methods that Buddha gave his followers and which have been passed down to us, we can travel the spiritual path with certainty.

When one takes refuge in the dharma, it is not that one simply assents to its truth, as if by reciting Buddha's teachings like a creed or pledging one's belief in them, one would somehow be saved. The teachings of the Buddha are not a creed but working instructions. If they are not put into practice, it would be like being given instructions on how to cook a meal plus all the ingredients and then leaving them untouched. There would be nothing for anyone to eat.

How does one know whether these instructions are reliable or not? The answer is that one can discern whether they are true because they can be tested with one's own reasoning. This testing is something one must do if one wants to take refuge in the dharma effectively. Buddha himself told his disciples not to rely on his teaching simply because he had taught it. He told them to take the teaching and test it to see if it works. As he said, 'One should be like a merchant who tests gold before buying it.' Buddha invited us to come, see, taste and test the dharma for ourselves. We must be certain that it is reliable if we are going to take refuge in it. The dharma is open to inspection and so one should take as much time as one needs to examine it.

3. The Sangha

The sangha is a suitable source of refuge since it is there to help and inspire us to succeed in our spiritual endeavours. The men and women in the sangha are our companions, the good friends with whom we walk the path of the dharma. They support us in times of difficulty and show us an example of how to practise the dharma. One should not think of the sangha as one particular organization. When one takes refuge in this third jewel one is taking refuge in the sangha of all those who have gone before one on the path, both those who have obtained deep realization and those ordinary members of the sangha who maintain their vows.

One might wonder if one really needs the jewel of the sangha? It may be thought that this third jewel is unnecessary, since if one just practises the dharma, that will be sufficient. However, in reality that approach does not seem to work. We need supportive friendship. It is not only that we are social beings, but we are actually interdependent beings, 'limbs of one life', as Shantideva puts it. Therefore, we should not see our spiritual practice as something entirely private. To do that would be to further imprison ourselves in the very cause of suffering; self-centredness. Practice of the Buddha's teachings involves seeing ourselves as social and interconnected, part of the world and part of the network of living beings. Where better to begin developing that sense of connectedness than in our spiritual practice? Then we can see our practice as part of the efforts which all these other men and women are making in practising Buddha's teachings. Without that attitude there is the danger of either isolation and loss of confidence, or of arrogance and self-obsession. Thus we can see how necessary it is to rely on the sangha.

The Motivation for Taking Refuge

It was said by the Buddha that the motivation behind any action is the crucial factor in determining the result of the action. This is equally the case with taking refuge. There are certain motives that must be present, at least to some degree, in order for taking refuge to be meaningful. These are fear, confidence and compassion.

Fear means the apprehension that if we do not take refuge in the Three Jewels, we could go on endlessly repeating the same mistakes that have been locking us into the cycle of suffering that we now experience. So it is the fear of that imprisonment that first compels us to take refuge, since the Three Jewels represent a real connection with emptiness, the ultimate ineffability at the heart of reality that transcends suffering.

Confidence or faith is the second motivation. In order to take refuge effectively we need to develop the confidence that the Three Jewels represent the only effective means of travelling the spiritual path successfully. Of course this does not mean blind faith, since that could not result in any sort of wisdom. Confidence is something that develops over time through understanding the teachings and gaining inspiration from hearing about the lives of the great masters of Buddhism.

Compassion is the third motivation. Although fear and confidence are essential in taking refuge, we should actually rely on the Three Jewels not for our benefit alone, but in order to bring benefit to others as well. If we take refuge in this way, then we have the best type of motivation.

The Method of Taking Refuge

How then do we relate to the Three Jewels when we take refuge? Regarding the Buddha, we should see him as **the teacher**. The dharma is to be understood as **the path** that leads to buddhahood. The sangha are the men and women who have entered the path before us and thus we take refuge in them as **companions on the path**.

In the Tibetan Buddhist tradition the act of taking refuge for the first time in the presence of either our lama or some senior member of the sangha marks the first step on the path. In this initial ceremony we repeat three times the actual verse of going for refuge that was taught by the Buddha himself.

> *I take refuge in the Buddha, most excellent among humans.*
> *I take refuge in the Dharma, most excellent in detachment.*
> *I take refuge in the Sangha, most excellent among assemblies.*

27

After this we are asked three times if we have understood the method of taking refuge and each time we reply in the affirmative. Following that, our teacher usually gives us a religious name symbolizing the very qualities that we will develop through taking refuge and cuts a lock of our hair to symbolize our joining of the sangha as lay followers (whereas a monk or nun would shave their heads completely).

However, taking refuge does not conclude with this initial ceremony. This just marks the beginning of the dharma path. All those who follow the Buddha's way repeat the verses of refuge and contemplate their meaning every day, this being the foundation for all their spiritual activities. Taking refuge is not simply a ceremony but an ever-deepening process in which year by year we grow in the very qualities embodied by the Three Jewels. Through doing this, such a time will come when we fully manifest the qualities of protection from suffering and become a source of refuge for others. So taking refuge is the first essential step in our practice of the Buddha's way.

The Training Associated with Taking Refuge

In Tibetan Buddhism it is said that there are 'three trainings' associated with the Three Jewels.

1. The Training Associated with Refuge in the Buddha

When we have taken refuge in the Buddha, we can no longer take refuge in other teachers or gods. This is a very important point, and one which people with little knowledge of Buddhism sometimes overlook. Buddhism is famous for its tolerance, as the Buddha has actually condemned needless partisanship. There has always been a relaxed attitude in Buddhism towards other religions. This is especially the case for those religions in which morality gives people a solid foundation for virtuous behaviour, because Buddha taught that virtue leads to happiness. Yet at the same time, we must understand that Buddha's teaching differs from other religious and philosophical traditions in certain key respects. If that were not the case, Buddha himself would hardly have bothered to teach. Neither would the great Buddhist masters have defended the dharma from its critics and opponents over the years.

Some people who are attracted to Buddhism in the West confuse tolerance with the mistaken belief that it is possible to blend together different religious traditions. We cannot do that, precisely because there are important differences. For example, one very obvious difference that distinguishes it from other major religious traditions is that Buddhism is a non-theistic tradition. It sees that no god is responsible for the creation of the world and that no Supreme Being maintains and looks after people and their destinies. Buddha taught that the world is the result only of actions, not the result of divine creation. This is what is meant by the doctrine of karma. Though there may well be powerful beings in other realms capable of exerting influence in our lives, it is impossible for any being to have created the universe, since it is inconceivable that any single unassisted cause could be the source of the endless diversity of the universe. Therefore, even with the best intentions in the world, we cannot take refuge in Buddha whilst also following a theistic tradition.

Just as the world cannot be both permanent and impermanent, so truth is not merely a matter of subjective opinion. The world is impermanent whether or not that is one's opinion. The modern trend of declaring that each person has his or her own equally valid truth is facile, mistaken and actually a not-so-subtle form of intolerance, since it is an excuse for never having to listen to anybody or question one's own beliefs.

2. The Training Associated with Refuge in the Dharma

The training associated with taking refuge in the dharma is described as refraining from harming other beings. Why is this so? The dharma is a medicine to cure the suffering of the world. If having taken refuge in it, we act with disregard for the happiness and spiritual welfare of others, harming them physically, verbally or mentally then we have contradicted the very quality of the dharma. How could we then declare that we are its followers?

The Buddha taught the abandonment of ten non-virtuous actions as follows:

> 1 *Killing, whether an unborn child or adult,*
>   *human or animal;*
> 2 *Stealing, whether by deception, force or*
>   *burglary;*
> 3 *Sexual misconduct;*
> 4 *Lying;*
> 5 *Slander;*
> 6 *Harsh speech;*
> 7 *Idle gossip;*
> 8 *Malevolence;*
> 9 *Covetousness;*
> 10 *Ignorance.*

3. The Training Associated with Refuge in the Sangha

Finally, the training associated with taking refuge in the sangha is that we should take only Buddhists as our spiritual companions. This can be related back to the point concerning the training associated with taking refuge in the Buddha. We should certainly respect those who follow other traditions. Yet, it should be evident that since the members of the sangha are those who help us with the practice of Buddha's dharma, those who follow other traditions cannot do so. That is the meaning of the third training.

Once we have taken refuge, we have begun on that great highway to realization of our innate spiritual potential. It is as if the centre of gravity in our life has shifted from focusing upon ultimately futile objects for security, happiness and contentment to focusing on what is meaningful. Through the Three Jewels we have connected with what is real. In fact at the most profound level the term 'Buddha' should not be confined only to the historical teacher. It is said in the Buddhist tradition that there are actually countless buddhas, since from time without beginning there have been those who have followed and completed the path to enlightenment. At the deepest level, however, 'buddha' refers to the capacity within us to awaken to the true nature of reality. That capacity is beginningless and endless and when discovered is known as the *dharmakaya*, the 'body of truth'. In the final analysis, this is the ultimate refuge and we have connected with it once we have participated in the ceremony of taking refuge. Each day when we repeat the verses of refuge we reconnect with that source of all wisdom and goodness.

Practising the Path

Once we have established a relationship with the principles of enlightenment that are embodied in the Three Jewels, we can begin to work with the teachings, systematically developing wisdom in our own life. It is taught that this process involves three facets; hearing, thinking and meditating. They are not to be understood as entirely distinct activities, but as connected with one another, each reinforcing the other. Vasubhandu, the great master of the fourth century AD, said, 'On the basis of moral behaviour one should then practise hearing, thinking and meditating.'

Hearing

Hearing, the first of the three facets, indicates that we should listen to the dharma, the words of the Buddha. The Buddha's teachings are vast in extent. In fact, they are so numerous that it would be foolish to think one could study them all before going any further on the spiritual path. On the other hand, neither should one think that it is correct to select particular teachings from the many translations of the Buddhist texts that are so prominently displayed in libraries and bookshops, thus teaching ourselves Buddhism. If we honestly consider this, we will understand that such a self-taught version of Buddhism would be entirely palatable to our prejudices and pre-conceptions, far removed from the true dharma, and therefore unable to effect any change in us for the better. Hence we need to connect with a teacher who can show us the teachings that will be most effective for us at the time, regardless of our preconceptions. We will explore the topic of the teacher in more detail in chapter 3.

Thinking

Secondly, we reflect on the teachings in order to internalize and digest them. 'Thinking' in this context therefore signifies the process of critical reflection, bringing to bear our common sense and life experience on the teachings we have heard. Whilst we may be very inspired when we hear the teachings, it is inevitable that we will also harbour doubts, hesitations and uncertainties. When the teachings are analysed, these are removed. It is that vital step of making the teachings personal, of transforming them from something external to us into a part of our very life. It is absolutely essential to do this, because unexamined teachings are teachings that are not part of us. We may have some superficial acceptance of them but if we have not truly developed confidence in them through the process of reflection they will be of little use when difficult circumstances arise in our life.

Meditating

Only when that process of digestion has occurred are we actually ready to meditate on the teachings. In the deepest sense meditation in Buddhism means to experience the reality of the teachings for ourselves. One might think that meditation simply means sitting quietly, attempting to calm the mind, but that is a somewhat narrow understanding. Meditation involves actualizing the teachings we have heard, turning them from mere ideas into experiences.

This three-fold process of listening to, thinking over and meditating on the teachings is ongoing, revolving again and again like a wheel. Having received teachings and reflected upon them, the subsequent stage of meditation itself encourages us to receive further teachings.

The Four Seals

One might ask what are the topics to which we should be listening and upon which we should be thinking and meditating. At the initial level of study and practice, there are four topics that are most important. They are the 'Four Seals', mentioned above:

> *All phenomena are impermanent;*
> *All phenomena are suffering;*

All phenomena are selfless;
Nirvana alone is peace.

Just as one can determine that a certain document has the authority of the monarch by the fact that it bears his seal, so the establishment of whether any particular teaching is Buddhist or not depends upon its conformity with the Four Seals. If a teaching contradicts the Four Seals, it is assuredly not a Buddhist teaching. Before we look at these in more detail, we should have some understanding of the context in which these teachings must be understood. The doctrine of rebirth is the essential element that underpins these teachings, so it is crucial to have some understanding of its significance.

Rebirth

According to my teachers the teaching on rebirth is the bedrock of the entire dharma, without which its practice makes little sense. If we do not take seriously the possibility that our positive and negative actions can lead to rebirth in human and non-human states, the dharma will only work for us in a very superficial manner. It may be the case that initially the teaching on rebirth is difficult for us to accept but, when it comes to the practice of dharma, we cannot 'pick and mix' teachings on the grounds of what we like or dislike. We cannot reject the Buddha's teachings on rebirth just because we do not feel attracted to them, yet at the same time seek to avail ourselves of other teachings more congenial to our tastes. This may be uncomfortable for those who would like to treat Buddhism merely as a set of techniques that can be applied in a kind of quasi-therapeutic situation, combining them with essentially non-spiritual or even highly materialistic views of the world. However, the Buddha's system is distinct from, and often radically divergent from, non-Buddhist systems.

This is not to imply we should take the opposite extreme of accepting the doctrine of rebirth unquestioningly. The Buddha's vision of the world is not something we must accept through blind faith. How could blind faith equate to the wisdom of enlightenment? There is a truth contained in the teachings that can only be discovered through critical reasoning and direct experience. It is, therefore, important to ask, 'How is it reasonable to believe in rebirth?' It seems that if we study this question without prejudice we will come to understand that rebirth is the only valid way to account for the reality of consciousness, as the great Buddhist masters of the past have explained in detail in many texts. Let us take a look at the rationality behind this understanding.

Consciousness is non-substantial and yet endowed with awareness. Such qualities cannot arise from a material basis, which is of course both substantial and devoid of awareness. For example, one might say that the material world is comprised of atoms, but it is obvious that atoms do not have any awareness. For consciousness to arise from them somehow would be a violation of the law of cause and effect. We cannot realistically expect consciousness to arise out of any number or arrangement of non-conscious atoms, any more than we could expect rice to come from barley seeds, or light to come from darkness. The cause of mind can only be something that has the same characteristics of formlessness and cognition. If we then ask from where does consciousness arise, the only possible answer is from the preceding moment of consciousness. Therefore, for consciousness to arise in this life it must be part of a continuum stretching back beyond the moment of conception to previous lives.

It is impossible for there to have been a 'first moment of consciousness', a time when at one moment there was no consciousness and in the next moment consciousness magically appeared.

Hence there is no logical alternative but to accept the existence of a continuum, or stream of consciousness, extending back over an infinite series of lifetimes. To posit anything else, such as the spontaneous creation of awareness from chemical substances, whether at conception or afterwards, or the creation of an immortal soul by the fiat of a creator God at the moment of conception, is to violate logic.

If there were no past and future lives, the whole structure and meaning of Buddha's teachings would be destroyed. What is more, if there were no future lives there would really be little point in practising dharma. One may as well just spend one's time during this life in abandonment to indulgence, since the consequences would be slight if all that happened at death was the complete termination of consciousness. Let us be clear about the significance of this. If there was simply extinction at the end of life, then we should all do as we please. How comforting to imagine that no matter how one has behaved, all that awaits one is the peaceful sleep of oblivion. Some people may have convinced themselves that they are 'tough minded' facing up to annihilation, yet the converse is true. Thus, it is those who believe in annihilation, and not those who believe in rebirth, who are really consoling themselves with something pleasant and fantastic. Nothing in nature disappears without trace or consequence.

The First Seal –
All Phenomena are Impermanent

Having understood something of this essential doctrine, we can now proceed to the Four Seals. To consider the first of the Four Seals, that all phenomena are impermanent, one could begin by opening one's eyes to the surrounding world. Nowhere in our environment is there anything that endures forever. From the greatest galaxy to the smallest atom, all things are subject to the inevitability of decay and destruction. We can see the continual process of change in the succession of the seasons, in the swift passing of years, months, weeks, days, hours and even minutes. In short, we should acknowledge that we move through a world that is itself nothing but movement.

Where is there anybody who has defied death? The greatest of heroes and even the greatest of saints have all passed away. Thus, there is no possibility that we can avoid death, our inevitable fate. How could we when impermanence is written in the very fabric of our body, comprised as it is merely of a temporary combination of fragile elements? Death is certain for us from the moment of our conception onwards, and as we have already discussed, it is not simply a termination of experience. This much is sure. What is uncertain is simply the precise time when death will befall us. Wherever I lay my gaze, all I can see is the fleeting nature of this world, exposing all my self-comforting delusions about permanence.

Whilst the impermanence of all things is in a sense quite obvious, we have perhaps been hiding away from its truth. We might intellectually assent to the fact of our impermanence, but that does not mean we have emotionally explored it. We have to investigate what it really means that I and all beings are impermanent, that we are certain to die, but at an unknown time.

Impermanence implies that most of the things in which we have so far sought meaning, happiness or security have been a waste of time. In fact, they are more than a waste of time, they are delusions that are robbing us of the opportunity to realize what is truly valuable, what is timeless, unborn and undying. To overcome our tendency to ignore impermanence, we have to research every corner of experience until a real internal conviction arises in us that everything is

37

transient and therefore cannot offer true security or happiness. No matter whether it is one's body, relationships, possessions, skills, acquisitions, opinions, or status, all of them are impermanent.

Furthermore, one should ask oneself, 'Which of the things that mean so much to me now can I take with me when I die?' The answer, of course, is none of them. Not one of them will be of the slightest use at the time of death. At death the mind and body separate. The body will return to the elements in one way or the other, but the mind will continue. However, the mind is formless, so it cannot carry with itself such things as houses, relationships, status or jobs. All that will accompany the mind at death will be the shadow of the actions one has performed during this and previous lives. It is that shadow of actions that will determine how the mind will next become embodied or 'reborn'.

So if I take to heart this first Seal, a revaluation of my life is inevitable. I cannot be content to fritter life away in escapist pleasures or vacuous dreams of power, because whatever I chase will eventually crumble, leaving me bereft of happiness and security. Far better that I turn now to the cultivation of that which is deathless; the enlightened mind, revealed to me by the dharma. Attachment to impermanent and essenceless things disappears, because one comes to know them for what they are.

The Second Seal – All Phenomena are Suffering

Now to investigate the truth of the second Seal, we can contemplate it under three headings: the suffering of suffering, suffering of change and suffering of conditionality. This will clarify exactly what the term 'suffering' means.

Newcomers are often misled by the emphasis on suffering in Buddhism. One might think that with so much attention paid to suffering, Buddhists must be very pessimistic and unhappy. Let us make it clear from the start that the term 'suffering' as used by the Buddha does not simply mean the moments of discomfort or unhappiness we sometimes experience. It refers to the whole gamut of experience, ranging from the most obvious types of suffering of body, such as sickness and pain, as well as sufferings of mind, such as great anguish, right up to the most subtle restlessness experienced even in very refined moments of experience. In short, suffering denotes any form of limitation in our life, or any way that we experience the world in anything less than its natural perfection.

In order to explain the meaning of three types of suffering, they are related to 'six realms' in which we can see each kind of suffering occur. The six realms are the six main forms of life into which beings are reborn through the power of karma.

1. The Suffering of Suffering

The suffering of suffering denotes the very undisguised types of suffering that are primarily experienced by those reborn into the so-called 'lower realms' of being – the hell, ghost and animal realms, caused by the ripening of actions committed through aggression, desire and ignorance, respectively. Although these realms are temporary, it is undeniable that the experience of beings locked within them is one of misery.

In the 'hell' realm beings experience repeated and terrible hallucinations of intense pain as the result of past acts of anger and violence. In the ghost realm the dominant form of misery is that of hallucinations of hunger, thirst and deprivation, which are themselves the outcome of previous lives characterized by avarice and grasping. Finally, animals, due to the accumulation of ignorance in previous lives, are oppressed by other animals and human kind.

We should contemplate the sufferings of beings in the lower realms because not only have we actually experienced them in our beginningless series of lives, we still carry the seeds of those realms within us in each moment of aggression, desire and ignorance. Who can deny that if we were born in such realms, there would be anything but a heap of misery? Since we cannot even bear even a slight pain in this human life, what would it be like to be locked in the misery that characterizes these realms?

2. The Suffering of Change

This second category of suffering generally refers to the type of suffering predominant in the human realm and the other 'upper realms', that is to say, the demi-god and god realms. It is best expressed by the observation that even when we acquire what seems to us to guarantee happiness, it inevitably proves unreliable. In fact reliance upon any form of happiness that is itself dependent upon impermanent conditions without doubt brings disappointment and frustration in its wake. It is not that there are no moments of happiness in human life but every time we fixate upon them we transform them into suffering. Furthermore, we should remind ourselves of the manner in which human existence is bounded by the suffering inherent in birth, ageing, sickness and death.

3. The Suffering of Conditionality

The final category of suffering is said to be the most disguised of the three, for it is only perceptible when we have refined our awareness through extensive meditation practice. When we have settled the mind sufficiently so that we can see beneath the surface of things, we will come to recognize that there is suffering inherent in our very reliance upon our body and mind as constituting a permanent self. This suffering occurs because in clinging to such a fragile construction, we are in conflict with how things truly are. We have been looking in the wrong places for happiness by clinging to the conditioned body and mind for succour.

The Third Seal – All Phenomena are Devoid of a Self

The third Seal is expressed in the axiom, 'All phenomena are devoid of a self.' The teaching of selflessness is well known as the most distinctive feature of Buddhism. As we have seen earlier, on the night of his enlightenment Buddha realized that the fundamental cause of suffering is the attachment to self. Such attachment comprises both the intellectual idea and the emotional conviction that there is within us an irreducible core, 'I' or 'me' which separates us from the rest of the world. To put it more technically, to believe in the reality of self is to believe that there is an independent, permanent and autonomous essence within our body and mind, or which in some way owns our body and mind. It is our determination to cling to this notion, not some external devil or god, which causes suffering. From the most trivial disappointment to the separation of body and mind experienced at the moment of death, all suffering is contingent upon clinging to self.

The tragedy of this is that the self, the root of suffering, is fictional. Buddha proposed that we examine the self by a clear and dispassionate analysis so that we can establish with certainty whether it is existent or not. This analysis is founded on simple calmness and attentiveness of mind. As to where we should seek this self, it should be sought in our experience, specifically our experience of the physical (body) and mental (mind). To put it more elaborately, in the categories of the Buddhist psychology it is the *five skandhas*, five 'heaps' or 'aggregates' that constitute our conditioned world from moment to moment. They are as follows:

> *Form or physicality;*
> *Sensations;*
> *Perceptions;*
> *Mental formations (encompassing motivation*
> *and other mental factors);*
> *Consciousness (signifying here the full*
> *apprehension of any object).*

If we examine these we will come to see that there is nothing in any one of these five aggregates, either singly or collectively, which can be identified as a self. They are all dependent upon internal and external circumstances. They are impermanent, since they are constantly changing. They are not self-controlling, so they have no autonomy. Thus the five skandhas are neither independent, permanent or autonomous.

We might then wish to claim that the self is not simply identical to, or somewhere within, the five heaps that comprise our body and mind, but that it is an agent that controls or owns them. However, we would have actually fallen into a ludicrous error, since we would be claiming that the self is somehow external to our mind and body. If this were so, then the 'self' would have no capacity to experience anything in our body and mind and thus would be utterly redundant.

Thus, no matter how much emotional investment has been made in the notion of self and no matter how long we have cultivated the idea of self, it has no more reality than any other type of tenaciously held delusion. All that is required to penetrate to the truth about the self is honest and clear analysis. There is nothing supernatural about it. In fact, to understand selflessness is relatively easy if we listen to and reflect over the presentations given by the Buddha. Of course, to go beyond a merely intellectual understanding requires intensive meditation practice. Yet as a basis for such practice the confidence provided by intellectual analysis is indispensable.

The Fourth Seal – Nirvana Alone is Peace

The term 'nirvana' is well known in Western culture and languages. The word actually signifies 'extinction', a fact which has been the cause of much confusion in the Western understanding of Buddhism. Etymologically, nirvana does indeed mean 'extinction' but the word here signifies the fact that in the apprehension of the true nature of reality the so-called 'fires' of desire, hatred and ignorance are extinguished. Once these fires have been blown out the suffering they produce is likewise brought to an end. Such is the bliss and peace of nirvana.

Buddha himself did not indulge in hyperbolic descriptions of nirvana. We can see that this was a wise tactic to prevent us identifying nirvana with any of the temporary conditioned states that comprise moments of apparent satisfaction in the realm of cyclical existence, or samsara.

Nirvana alone is peace. How could it be otherwise? Where there is attachment to self, there is never peace, but always the unsatisfied yearning produced by the sense of incompleteness and insecurity

43

that is part and parcel of self-interest. When that restless yearning ceases, there is all-encompassing bliss. So nirvana is not an alternative reality or a heaven realm. It is actually being in the natural state itself, devoid of all fictional experiences projected by self-clinging. As it is the natural state, it is unchanging. Nirvana is that which is unproduced, uncreated and undying. It is that alone for which one should strive.

THREE

THE SPECIAL PATH –
Mahayana

The Three Jewels and the Four Seals are common to every tradition of Buddhism, for they are the very teachings that make Buddhism unique as a religious tradition. Now we will consider that which is distinctive to the Buddhism of Tibet and which forms the most advanced part of the spiritual path. Earlier we saw how Buddha's teachings may be divided into the 'small' and 'great' vehicles, the hinayana and mahayana. It is this second category of teaching that we will now consider.

The Compassion of Mahayana

What is it that distinguishes the mahayana from the hinayana? The most important distinction lies in their respective motivation. We could practise the common teachings of Buddhism with the aim of simply liberating ourselves alone from suffering but such a motivation is a restricted one. Since it is the case that everybody in this world is subject to suffering, how can we isolate ourselves from others and their difficulties? In the mahayana it is taught that we should see ourselves as intimately connected with all other sentient beings and thus as having a responsibility to help free them from suffering. This intimate connection with all others is not a mere sentimental idea but is actually rooted in the way things are.

The cycle of existence can have no first cause, since things cannot simply arise or be wished into existence out of nothingness. Thus whatever exists at any time must have preceding causes. The cycle of existence is therefore beginningless and sentient beings must have been revolving within it from time without beginning. As this means that we have all taken an infinite number of births we can conclude that all beings have been related to us as parents (and indeed related to us in an infinite number of other ways also) in innumerable lifetimes.

This point can be seen in the following episode from the life of Buddha's disciple Katyayana. One day while he was out on his alms-round, Katyayana encountered a man who was sitting with his child on his lap. This man was eating a fish while at the same time throwing stones at a dog that wanted the fish bones. As a great master of meditation Katyayana was endowed with clairvoyance and thus saw that the fish was in fact the rebirth of the man's own father, the dog was his mother and the child was an enemy whose life he had taken in a previous existence.

Just as we owe an incalculable debt to our present parents for their kindness, protection and nurturing, so we must acknowledge that we are equally indebted to all beings, no matter how distant they might appear to be from us during this present life. Thus we should enter the spiritual path to bring liberation from suffering for all beings, our previous parents. Such is the compassion of the mahayana.

One might then ask who has the ability to show others the way to liberation. The mahayana answer is that only a buddha has the ability, because only a buddha is fully awakened from the spell of the ego. He therefore possesses the limitless perspective of wisdom, the utterly uncompromising inclusiveness of compassion and the boundless energy and power to benefit others. So, just as one who wants to cure peoples' sicknesses trains to become a doctor we should train to become a buddha.

This resolution to become a buddha for the benefit of all sentient beings is known as *bodhichitta* and it is this which is the motivating force that animates the mahayana. Once bodhichitta has arisen within us, we have entered into the path to buddhahood and can be known as a *bodhisattva*, a being destined for enlightenment.

The mahayana teaches us to put aside concerns about our own liberation in favour of the vaster concern to benefit others. Yet it is actually not possible to achieve liberation unless we do just that. Buddha taught that the cause of suffering is privileging self. Therefore if we ignore the needs of others, we ourselves cannot escape the cycle of suffering. Thus we find the paradox that in order to benefit oneself one has to give up all self-clinging and self-cherishing through bodhichitta, a fact that is displayed in the story of how Buddha himself entered the spiritual path.

It is said that, many lives previous to his enlightenment, the Buddha was born in a hell where the beings were tortured by pulling wagons. He was harnessed to a wagon with another person called Kamarupa, but the two of them were too weak to move their vehicle. The guards of this particular hell beat them with red-hot weapons but all to no avail.

It then occurred to the Buddha, 'Even with two of us together we cannot get the wagon to move, and each of us is suffering as much as the other. I will pull it and suffer alone, so that Kamarupa can be freed.'

He said to the guards, 'Put his harness over my back, so I can pull the car on my own.'

However, the guards were enraged. 'There is no way to prevent beings from experiencing the effects of their own actions,' they said, and beat him about the head with their clubs.

Nevertheless, due to the power of his selfless thought, Buddha was immediately released from hell and reborn in a celestial realm. It is said that this was how he first began to benefit others and travel to enlightenment.

The Wisdom of Mahayana

So far we have mentioned bodhichitta only as it arises out of com-passion. This is often referred to as *conventional* bodhichitta. However, there is also bodhichitta as it arises through wisdom. This second type is called *ultimate* bodhichitta. The two forms of bodhi-chitta correspond to the two ways of looking at the world taught in the mahayana. The *conventional* way is the ordinary, everyday way of looking at the world in which things are not examined as to their real nature. From this point of view appearances are unexamined and taken to be as they seem. However, as we saw when we were discussing the teachings on selflessness, how things appear to be and how they really are, are not necessarily the same thing. By examining how phenomena are in reality, we come to penetrate their true nature. This is the ultimate bodhichitta.

In chapter 2 we saw that the five skandhas comprising the body and mind are without any nature of their own. However, this is only a partial understanding of how things are, because we have restricted our analysis to ourselves as individuals. In the mahayana the lack of any abiding essence is actually seen as true of all phenomena, from the tiniest atom to the most subtle moment of consciousness. All phenomena that make up the world are empty of intrinsic nature. This does not mean that their lack of intrinsic nature implies that they are merely nothing. When we see that all phenomena are without essence, we simultaneously see that all things are actually

49

interdependent rather than non-existent. Whatever exists owes its existence to the coming together of a multiplicity of causes and conditions and a multiplicity of parts. This is the 'dependent origination' of all phenomena and it is this which creates the appearance of a solidity in the world. However, that solidity is nothing more than an appearance. When analysed, the supposedly solid object is seen as devoid of solidity or essence precisely because it is appearing out of this seemingly magical combination of causes and conditions. This understanding is what is known as the recognition of *emptiness*. Perceiving phenomena in this way is ultimate bodhichitta, the wisdom aspect of bodhichitta.

These twin facets of bodhichitta are the two crucial teachings that underlie the mahayana. Conventional bodhichitta is the vast compassion for the benefit of others through which the grip of selfishness is diminished. Ultimate bodhichitta is the profound insight into the nature of all things, which also cuts through our fixation upon self because it finds no ground for self or other to exist. Thus the two bodhichittas are not contradictory but complementary ways to excise self-clinging.

Meditating on Bodhichitta

In mahayana there is a series of contemplative exercises to develop the two bodhichittas. It is usually easier to concentrate firstly on conventional bodhichitta. This itself arises through the development of love and compassion respectively, the wish that all beings be pervaded by happiness and the wish that all beings be freed from suffering. These preliminary steps trigger off in us the sense of universal responsibility that is the very crux of bodhichitta. In order to stabilize this attitude once it has arisen we might find it useful to train in the techniques known as 'equalizing oneself with others' and 'exchanging oneself with others'. In the first of these we dissolve our self-obsession in the understanding that every single being is equal to oneself in his or her drive for happiness and wish to avoid suffering. In the second technique one reverses one's habitual concepts of self and other by treating others as oneself and oneself as another.

I am used to calling one particular combination of body and mind 'I' and other combinations of body and mind 'you' but why should I do this? Wouldn't it be just as valid to think of these as 'I' – to put myself in other's shoes? By this creative re-imagination of who I am I can step out of the narrow confines of my ego into the spaciousness and warmth of compassion.

By cherishing others with the same degree of intensity that one had previously reserved for oneself, one collapses the egocentric perception of the world. Such is the way to develop the good-heartedness of mahayana.

To extend this bodhichitta exercise to everyday life and thus to transform our actions we should ask ourselves in every situation, 'What good am I?' Whenever we meet somebody we should ask ourselves, 'What can I do for you?' Even small actions like opening doors for other people, or actually listening to others before stating one's own views are powerful means of creating the room for bodhichitta to arise.

If we are fearful that we might experience problems through working for others we should recall the words of Shantideva:

> *Not only nirvana, but also all happiness in this*
> *world comes from exchanging oneself for others.*

51

Once conventional bodhichitta has arisen, we can embark upon the stages of developing ultimate bodhichitta. In the first stage of this we focus upon the meditation of *shamatha*, 'calm-abiding', in order to attain stillness and attentiveness. Only when we have achieved such one-pointedness of mind are we able to practise *vipashyana*, 'insight', in which we investigate the empty nature of both phenomena and mind.

In the first stage of vipashyana we analyse the relationship between mind and external phenomena. Is it really the case that visual forms, sounds and other sense objects are external to and separate from our mind, or is it that they are simply appearances like those in a dream? Through the repeated investigation of this question in meditation we come to the conclusion that all appearances are actually arising from mind and have no other basis. In this way we have reached the level of insight into reality taught in the chittamatra school of philosophy.

However, this understanding is insufficient for liberation since we may be trapped by the view that the mind itself is some kind of sub-stantial reality so we should enter into the second stage of vipashyana. Here we search for the nature of mind, asking our-selves, 'What is mind's colour, shape and location?' Yet, the more we strive in this way, the more we discover the mind's unfindability since it has neither colour, shape, location or any other characteris-tics by which it can be grasped. Thus, one cannot assert that the mind exists as a substantial entity, but at the same time it is not a mere non-existent entity since it is, as we have seen, the basis of all appearances which are themselves the manifestation of mind's perceptive faculty or 'luminosity' as it is known. One must conclude that mind is 'unelaborated', that is to say it cannot be reduced to dualistic categories such as existence and non-existence. It cannot be grasped by thought or label. Such realization is in accord with the madhyamaka, the supreme school of mahayana philosophy.

Nagarjuna, founder of the madhyamaka philosophical school   53

Finally, by uniting shamatha and vipashyana we rest in the realization of the non-dual nature of reality beyond all concepts. Our illusions about the world dissolve in the all-embracing wisdom that arises naturally in every situation.

Since these teachings on the two bodhichittas are so vital to the mahayana practitioner, one needs a clear and extensive understanding of them. For this it is helpful to study the classical works of the mahayana composed by such masters as Chandrakirti and Shantideva. In their texts we are shown the step-by-step way to develop authentic compassion and wisdom. If one enters this path, one should be sure to ask one's teachers for instructions in these works.

The Two Types of Mahayana

Within the mahayana itself we can distinguish two divisions which may be called the ordinary and extraordinary mahayana respectively. The first of these is a graduated form of practice known also as the *paramitayana*, the 'Vehicle of Perfections'. The second is a very skilful, rapid form of practice also known as the *mantrayana*, the 'Way of Mantras', and even more commonly referred to as *vajrayana*.

The paramitayana can be understood as a path on which we endeavour to gather the 'accumulations' of merit and primordial wisdom which are the causes that will eventually lead to the fruit of buddhahood itself. These two accumulations are collected through the transcendental virtues known as the six perfections. These are:

> *Giving;*
> *Moral discipline;*

Patience;
Energy;
Meditation;
Wisdom.

The vajrayana, the 'Indestructible Vehicle', may be described by contrast as a way of practising which, instead of focusing on gathering the right causes for enlightenment, actually takes enlightenment as something already present within us. Therefore it is a path of the most direct nature imaginable. The Hevajra tantra says, 'All beings are already buddhas but this is temporarily obscured.' This gets right to the heart of the difference between the paramitayana and the vajrayana.

The Vajrayana

As we have mentioned earlier, the origins of the vajrayana lie in the tantras taught by the Buddha. The term 'tantra' means 'continuum' and signifies the continuum of being which links an ordinary person and a buddha. Due to this continuum enlightenment with all its powers is nothing more than the unveiling of the wisdom mind that exists within both buddhas and sentient beings. It is said, therefore, that the only difference between a buddha and a sentient being is that a buddha recognizes the nature of his or her mind but a sentient being does not. If we do not recognize the nature of our mind, we will misread the appearances that originate from its luminosity as external to ourselves. Thus we create the cycle of suffering, samsara, simply through not recognizing mind's nature. If we come to see mind as it truly is, a union of emptiness and luminosity, we immediately become a buddha. This principle is the foundation of the whole of vajrayana.

The Four Sets of Tantra

As there are many hundreds of tantras, in order to help people practise those which are appropriate to their needs, early vajrayana masters grouped them into four sets. It is only necessary to explain them here in brief.

The kriya tantras place most emphasis on external, ritual activity, such as making offerings to the deities of vajrayana and practising pure conduct.

The charya tantras are similar to kriya but give more emphasis to meditation.

The yoga tantras focus upon meditation alone.

The anuttara tantras ('supreme' tantras) provide many extraordinarily subtle means of acquiring realization which are not found in the other tantra sets, most importantly the techniques of the development and completion stages.

Entering Vajrayana

Before entering onto the vajrayana path it is useful to consider whether one has the necessary aptitude and appropriate conditions. Furthermore, one must find a suitably qualified master, because his or her guidance is absolutely imperative in the vajrayana. The characteristics that the vajrayana teacher must possess will be explained later.

Virupa, great adept of vajrayana

Why do we need a teacher in vajrayana? It is because we cannot take up any form of tantric practice without first receiving the relevant initiation from a vajrayana master. That is why, incidentally, any thought of practising vajrayana simply by reading books containing tantric material is utterly misconceived. In fact it seems that if one attempts to do this, it will not only result in a lack of progress but will actually be very damaging to oneself. Initiation is the gateway to vajrayana. In order for a tantric master himself to be able to bestow an initiation, he must also have acquired the initiation from his own master. This line of transmission is called the *lineage* of the teaching. Without that lineage, the spiritual power of the teaching will have been dissipated. All Buddhist teachings must have a lineage, but initiation is characteristic only of vajrayana. Receiving initiation is the gateway to any level of vajrayana practice. The initiations bestowed by tantric masters are essentially ritual embodiments of the transference of meditative realization.

In an initiation the master bestows upon us the spiritual authority to meditate on a particular deity, or 'yidam' as it is known in Tibetan. Such deities are emanations of the enlightened qualities of the buddhas who are able to appear in whatever way necessary to help beings.

Since every buddha has by their nature realized selflessness they are not restricted to any particular form but able to manifest in whatever form is appropriate. Thus in initiations we are introduced to buddhas as they appear in the form of deities. Of course one must acknowledge that Buddhism is a non-theistic tradition and, therefore, when we talk about deities, it is not implying that a buddha is actually some sort of god. Buddha taught that all beings are empty of essence so that there is no such thing as a permanent god who can create a truly existent universe.

At a profound level we can understand the nature of the deities in the following way. In the vajrayana it is taught that the ultimate nature of reality is not a mere emptiness but that in fact this emptiness is endowed with luminosity, the very basis of all appearances. These expressive powers of emptiness are the deities upon which we meditate if we enter vajrayana. Ultimately, therefore, the deities of vajrayana dwell within us and by meditation upon them we discover the inner buddha.

Two subsidiary forms of transmission accompany the bestowal of initiation. First, one receives the *lung*, 'reading transmission', which is an introduction to a text that can be used as the tantric practice. Secondly, one must receive the *tri*, 'instructions', where specific guidance on how to carry out the practice is given.

The Qualifications of the Vajrayana Master

It is necessary for us to rely upon a fully qualified vajrayana master, for if we entrust ourselves to someone who is unqualified and unable to communicate the teachings properly, we are likely to come to grief. It would be like entrusting ourselves to a blind man when wandering near a cliff. Such a guide may not be ill-intentioned but if he lacks the knowledge of dharma he cannot point us in the right direction. Furthermore, if he is devoid of spiritual experience he cannot remove our obscurations. As Patrul Rinpoche put it, such a master is like a flour mill that is so soft it cannot grind the corn.

As to the qualities a master must possess, in The Fifty Verses on the Guru' Bhavideva declares:

He should be skilled in the methods of mantras　　　　59

*and tantras, full of loving compassion and be
expert in the scriptures. He should have full
expertise in the series of ten subjects (of tantric
practice), be skilled in the drawing of mandalas
and in explaining the tantras. He should be full of
faith, and have his senses fully under control.*

Thus, a master must be equipped with both extensive learning and
genuine compassion. It is also said that he or she must be free from
pride, anger and spite and be endowed with a degree of concern for
his of her disciples similar to that felt by a parent for his or her child.
Furthermore, the lama must have received the full range of
vajrayana initiations and teachings from an unbroken lineage and
maintain all his vows flawlessly. In addition, he must have accomplished extensive retreats and obtained signs of success in his practice, such as blessings from the deities.

Even when we have some idea of the qualities of a lama, it is not
immediately obvious when someone possesses them. As it says in
the Fifty Verses, 'The prudent person should first proceed to an
examination of the master.' We have to examine a prospective
teacher carefully before becoming his student. In this respect it is
important to know that every genuine vajrayana master is part of an
unbroken lineage, that is to say he or she has received the teachings
in an unbroken succession going back to the Buddha himself. In
fact, unless their own teachers passed away long before, he or she
would have been authorized or empowered directly by their master
or masters to transmit the teachings. Self-appointed gurus are by
their very nature to be avoided, because whatever else they may be,
they do not have the blessings of the lineage but speak only from
the narrowness of their own perception.

One must be aware, too, of the dangers of infatuation with an apparently charismatic figure. An authentic lama directs people beyond his personality, towards the teachings for which he is merely a vehicle. As Buddha himself enjoined, 'Do not rely on the person but on the teaching.' This caution makes it easier to understand the real nature of devotion developed by the student in a correct relationship with a vajrayana master.

It is said in the tantras that if one wishes to gain realization, it is necessary to receive the blessing of the lama. To obtain these blessings the student must generate a devotion towards his master as the very embodiment of the buddhas. Before discussing this further it might be useful here to distinguish the type of relationship with the teacher one has in the sutra (non-tantric) teachings and the relationship one has with a tantric master. In the sutra teachings one's master is someone who imparts the philosophical texts of the hinayana and mahayana and gives instruction in the necessary conduct of a bodhisattva. This kind of teacher is known in Tibetan as the *gewai zhe-nyen*, 'spiritual friend'. He resembles the Buddha in his kindness and spiritual wisdom and, therefore, one develops towards him a trust born out of critical examination and engagement with his teachings. When one develops a relationship with a tantric master, beginning with an initiation, the relationship and role of the teacher has a deeper and more committed tone to it. To signify this in the tantras the teacher is called the 'vajra master'. He is not to be regarded as simply *like* a buddha as in the mahayana but in fact as *being* a buddha.

In 'The Fifty Verses' it says:

> *By pleasing the lama one gains all spiritual accomplishments, because the lama is in fact the Buddha.*

This point confirms once again that it is not the personality that is the crucial element in the status of the lama but the non-personal element described here as the Buddha. A lama is only a lama in as much as he or she has moved aside so that the 'Buddha', in the sense of the primordial wisdom that exists within him, is able to speak through him to the disciples and so awaken the primordial wisdom that lies within them. A connection exists between ordinary beings and that wisdom from the moment we take initiation from a lama. Developing contempt for the lama breaks that connection, since he is the one who establishes it by allowing the wisdom to manifest in him. That is why without the relationship with the lama being maintained, no progress is possible on the vajrayana path. For this reason there are many teachings on how the disciple who has received initiation should act towards the lama.

The manner in which students should behave towards the lama is often summed up in what has been termed 'the three ways of pleasing the lama'. These are:

1.　*To support the lama in whatever way one can;*

2.　*To look beyond the lama's personality and develop a perception of him or her as a buddha, thus creating in oneself the necessary openness to the liberating teachings;*

3.　*To accomplish the instructions of the lama.*

By behaving in this way we can be of the greatest benefit to all since we, like our lama before us, will progress along the vajrayana path and so come to be the very embodiment of all the qualities of wisdom and compassion of a buddha. In addition, the lama's own task is fulfilled through us reaching such an accomplishment and therefore this is the supreme way to please the lama.

One might ask, 'Is it the case that one must only receive teachings from one lama or should one go to many?' It is a point well worth clarifying. If one looks at the example of Tibetans, a pattern emerges in which one sees that in every serious spiritual practitioner's life there are one or two masters who are of much greater significance than any others. These are the masters upon whom the practitioner has relied throughout his life, not just for the formal transmission of the teachings but also for the invaluable instructions that give personal direction. In many cases, however, this exemplary practitioner will also have received some formal teachings from other lamas, perhaps his lama's masters or other great masters from his tradition. In this respect, he has not shopped around indiscriminately from master to master (a sure way of putting off any genuine spiritual engagement) but rather has seen the different teachers on his spiritual path as extensions of his principal lama's activity. He will, in most cases, have been recommended to take a particular teaching from one of these other masters by his own lama. In this way the essential sanity and groundedness of his or her spiritual practice is preserved.

Vows and Pledges of Vajrayana

All levels of Buddhist practice entail commitments, vows and pledges to uphold certain types of behaviour. The vows that accompany the common foundations of dharma and allow us to practise them effectively are determined by whether one is a lay person or a monk or nun. The vows of a lay person are primarily the five precepts of not killing, stealing, lying, practising sexual misconduct or becoming intoxicated. The monastic vows are far more extensive.

The lay and monastic vows of the common foundations are generally known as the *pratimoksha* vows. When entering into the mahayana through the compassionate motivation of bodhichitta, one takes what is known as the 'bodhisattva vow'. This is the commitment to work ceaselessly for the sake of others and avoid everything that would damage that altruistic behaviour. In the vajrayana the vows and pledges to uphold the appropriate behaviour and view are known as *samaya*, 'sacred commitment'.

The purpose of samaya is to allow us to retain the sacred outlook to which we are introduced by our tantric master at the time of initiation. We must remain true to this, or we will obstruct the possibility of success on the vajrayana path. Here we will simply list the principle vows found in the two higher sets of tantras and expressed as a commitment to avoid 'fourteen root downfalls'.

- *Do not have contempt for one's tantric master.*

- *Do not contradict the words of the Buddha.*

- *Do not take one's tantric brothers and sisters as enemies.*

- *Do not abandon loving-kindness towards any sentient being.*

- *Do not abandon bodhichitta.*

- *Do not have contempt for one's own or another's path.*

- *Do not reveal tantric secrets.*

- *Do not despise the body.*

- *Do not doubt the intrinsic purity of all phenomena.*

- *Do not display affection towards evil beings.*

- *Do not grasp at the nameless.*

- *Do not cause people to lose their faith in the dharma.*

- *Do not reject samaya substances.*

- *Do not despise women whose nature is wisdom.*

If someone wished to practise only the sutra teachings of the hinayana and mahayana there would be no need for him to take initiations, perform vajrayana meditations or hold the vajrayana vows. Yet those who do enter the vajrayana certainly cannot give up their earlier vows of the hinayana and mahayana, for the vows and pledges of the lesser vehicles are actually indispensable elements of the vajrayana. If one abandons such vows as not killing, or gives up bodhichitta, then one's vajrayana career is also destroyed. This is because the vajrayana is not entirely separate from the hinayana and mahayana, but their culmination. It is often said that the vajrayana is like the golden roof on top of the temple of hinayana and mahayana.

So one enters the vajrayana through the receipt of initiations, and then the upholding of sacred commitment ensures that the blessing received during initiation remains effective and wholesome within us. The third essential element is the practice of the vajrayana meditation systems.

The Development and Completion Stages

There are countless systems of meditations, or *sadhana*, in each of the four sets of tantras. Many of these lead to the acquisition of so called 'mundane siddhis' (powers) such as long life, prosperity and pacification of harmful forces. However, it is said that only the sadhanas of the anuttara tantra lead to the ultimate siddhi, *mahamudra*, 'The Great Seal', in this very lifetime. With this power of primordial wisdom one has achieved enlightenment itself.

There are two principal phases in all anuttara tantra cycles, namely the development stage which focuses upon luminosity and the completion stage which focuses upon emptiness. In the development stage, by visualizing ourselves as the deity, equipped with entourage and palace, we transform all appearances, internal and external, into the pure realm of the buddhas and simultaneously dissolve our ordinary sense of self in divine pride. This pride is nothing to do with egotism since it arises out of the recognition of our primordial identity with the buddha nature. There are numerous anuttara tantra deities but amongst those which are most commonly practised are Hevajra, Chakrasamvara, Vajrabhairava and the goddess Vajrayogini. Each of these cycles of practice has many subdivisions, for instance both Vajrayogini and Hevajra have several associated yogas.

The confidence engendered by the development stage allows us to practise the second stage, the completion stage. The techniques of this stage are usually classified as either with or without signs. The completion stage meditations without signs involve simply meditating directly on the nature of mind. The practices with signs, by contrast, revolve around the subtle body. The subtle body is the non-physical system located within the ordinary gross body of the four elements which links mind to physical processes. It is comprised primarily of three facets; the channels (or pathways), winds (currents of energy that flow along the channels) and the white and red drops (male and female vital substances) located at either end of the central channel. Completion stage techniques allow us to control the flow of energy in the subtle body. When the winds are gathered into the central channel, this precipitates the unification of the male and female drops. At the instant of this unification comes the dissolution of all dualistic experiences in great bliss.

The Superiority of Vajrayana

Why is it that vajrayana is said to be superior to the ordinary mahayana? It is important to understand this because one might be discouraged from entering into it when it might seem to be too complex or arduous. In the tantras themselves four superiorities are spelled out.

1. It points out the view in the most direct manner

'View' here means the nature of reality as it is. In non-tantric systems ultimate reality is not pointed out directly by the teacher but explained through reasoning and analogies that allow us to understand that all phenomena are empty. This is the view with which one meditates. This understanding however is only conceptual, not the actual experience of naked reality itself. In the vajrayana, during the course of the initiation or subsequently whilst practising meditation, one can experience the seeing of reality face-to-face, rather than merely understanding it with concepts.

67

2. It has many skilful means

This means that the vajrayana has far more techniques than the non-tantric system for achieving one's aims. These include practices that allow us to gather very quickly the factors that will help us easily to practise the dharma path, such as intelligence, prosperity and health. It also has, as we have already seen, the supremely skilful practices of anuttara tantra, which allow us to achieve complete realization in this very life.

3. It is without difficulties

In the non-tantric teachings the things we encounter in the world, the objects of the senses, are seen as to be avoided or even dangerous because it is entanglement with sense objects that causes us to remain in suffering. The vajrayana approach is based upon the underlying purity of all things, so that even the most powerful objects of the senses need not be shunned. Precisely because they are inherently pure, they do not need to be abandoned. They can be utilized as part of the very process of awakening. That makes the vajrayana so much easier in the sense that it does not require austerity.

4. It is for those with the sharpest faculties

It is said that those practitioners with most skill can achieve buddhahood in this very life through vajrayana.

Therefore we have in Tibetan Buddhism an option of following the slow but safe path of the six perfections or the swift and skilful path of the vajrayana. Making this decision requires us to have at least the knowledge set out in this chapter for our decision to be well based. We will return to some of the points touched upon here in subsequent chapters, beginning in the next chapter with the schools of Tibetan Buddhism.

FOUR

THE SCHOOLS OF
Tibetan Buddhism

To understand how the schools of Tibetan Buddhism developed it is helpful to trace their development out of the activity of particular masters and their disciples. In the previous chapters we have already seen the importance of the lineage of teaching. It is through such unbroken lines of transmission that the major and minor schools of Tibetan Buddhism came into being. Buddha had given so many different practices to lead beings to enlightenment that clusters of gurus and disciples were able to specialize in one particular set of teachings, for which perhaps they alone held the transmission. Thus the schools represent the culmination of a long process of development carried on by such groups, each of whom transmitted a series of instructions from the Indian inheritance. It is possible to distinguish nine schools of practice in Tibet, although over the course of time four of them became dominant, each eventually establishing its own fairly separate existence in its monasteries, retreat-centres, colleges and supporting lay communities. The four schools are the Nyingma, Sakya, Kagyu and Gelug. Of these, the Nyingma derives from the early transmission period of Buddhism in Tibet in the eighth century and the other three derive from the 'new transmission period' from the eleventh century onwards. *Nyingma* actually means 'the ancient ones' and that tradition is known as the school of the ancient translation period, whereas the others are collectively known as the *sarma* or new tantric schools.

Nyingma – The School of the Ancient Transmission Period

In the late eighth century, as we have seen, there was a collaboration between King Trison Detsen and his two Indian masters – the philosopher and abbot Shantarakshita, and the peerless tantric master Padmasambhava, the 'Precious Guru'. It is from this collaboration that the lineages of teachings comprising the Nyingma tradition may be said to originate. The tantric teachings of Padmasambhava are therefore especially important in the Nyingma school. It is worth noting in passing that Nyingma was not regarded as an individual tradition until some centuries later when the schools of the new transmission period became established.

The Early Masters

The early practitioners who we can designate as belonging to the Nyingma school were the *ngakpas*, 'tantric yogins', who mastered and preserved the oral transmission teachings of Guru Padmasambhava. They continued the practice of Buddhism right through the dark period of Tibet's history, between the ninth and the eleventh centuries, and thus ensured the unbroken transmission of the teachings despite the suppression of the monasteries. They include such adepts as Nyak Yeshe Zhonnu and Nubchen Sangye Yeshe.

Beginning in the eleventh century, a revitalizing stream of teachings began to appear in the form of the so-called 'treasures' deposited by Padmasambhava (see chapter 1). From then on the Nyingma school was adorned and strengthened by the revelations of over one hundred *tertons*, 'treasure revealers', who not only discovered these treasures but practised and transmitted them to disciples.

Longchenpa

The greatest figure in the history of the Nyingma school after Padmasambhava was Longchen Rabjam (1308–63). Having mastered the teachings of all the different streams of Buddhism existent in Tibet during his lifetime, he dedicated himself to a series of extremely arduous retreats and eventually won supreme enlightenment. Longchenpa composed over 250 works but of special importance is his delineation of the *nine* vehicles of dharma, a more precise categorization than the usual three-fold 'hinayana, mahayana and vajrayana' division that we have seen. The nine-fold division of dharma is as follows:

1. *Sravakayana*
2. *Pratyekabuddhayana*
3. *Bodhisattvayana*
4. *Kriya tantra*
5. *Upa tantra*
6. *Yoga tantra*
7. *Maha-yoga tantra*
8. *Anu-yoga tantra*
9. *Ati-yoga tantra*

These first two vehicles belong to the hinayana. The former is for those who wish to practise amongst the sangha (*sravakas*, or 'hearers') and the latter is for those who wish to practise alone in retreat (*pratyekabuddhas*, or 'solitary realizers'). The bodhisattvayana corresponds to the 'ordinary mahayana', the path of the six perfections explained in the previous chapter. Kriya, upa and yoga tantras are the three 'outer' tantras. These may be said to be equivalent to the first three tantra sets of the 'new transmission' schools, also explained in the previous chapter, although where previously there was the 'charya' tantra set, here there is the 'upa' tantra. The maha-, anu-, and ati-yoga tantras are the three 'inner' tantras, which are not found in the new transmissions schools but have similarities to the anuttara tantra.

Dzok chen, the 'Great Perfection', the crowning glory of the Nyingma teachings, is found in the ati-yoga tantra vehicle, the highest of the nine. Longchenpa ensured that dzok chen would not only be understood within the Nyingma school as the teaching which leads to Buddhahood in this very life but also that it would receive respect and appreciation from the masters of other schools. Thus, Longchenpa was crucial for the preservation of dzok chen.

Later Masters

The Nyingma tradition has been blessed by many other remarkable masters. Rigdzin Jigme Lingpa (1729–97) continued the work of Longchenpa, in particular through his discovery of the mind treasure teachings known as the *Longchen Nyingthig*, 'the heart essence of Longchen'. Another great teacher was Patrul Rinpoche (1808–87), one of the most beloved figures in Tibetan Buddhism. Perhaps more than any other Tibetan master, Patrul carried his teachings into the hearts of ordinary people through his uncompromising, down-to-earth approach, which caused him to shun monastic tradition and prestige.

On one occasion Patrul Rinpoche was travelling incognito in Eastern Tibet, when he met a poor woman with her family who were on their way to attend teachings given by a high Nyingma lama. Patrul Rinpoche decided to accompany her and help with her children. Finally, they reached the place where the teachings were to be given. Patrul Rinpoche excused himself, saying he had some business to which he must attend. Later that same day when she attended the teachings the poor woman was astonished to find that her humble travelling companion was none other than the great Patrul Rinpoche now seated on the throne bestowing teachings.

Of the four major schools of Buddhism in Tibet, the Nyingma has been the least monastic; down to the present day many of the leading figures have actually been lay yogins. Indeed, almost all treasure revealers have been such. In the sixteenth and seventeenth centuries, monasticism did begin to flourish within the Nyingma tradition in such monasteries as Mindrol Ling and Dorje Drak. In time six major Nyingma monasteries, each with many branches, were established in Tibet. Nevertheless, the Nyingma tradition retained a strong emphasis upon the role of the lay yogin and it is perhaps for this reason that the school, though it produced many distinguished scholars and monks, never lost the intense vitality of its meditative tradition.

The Great Perfection

According to the Nyingma tradition the first human teacher of dzok chen was the master known in Tibet as Garab Dorje, though in fact he hailed from Oddiyana rather than Tibet. It is clear that Garab Dorje received the transmission of dzok chen from the trans-historical Buddha Vajrasattva and in turn transmitted it to his disciple Manjushrimitra. Through him it reached Shri Singha and then Jnanasutra, Vimalamitra and Padmasambhava himself. The latter two figures were responsible for the arrival of dzok chen in Tibet.

Dzok chen is often described not so much as an actual practice but rather as a state; i.e. the state of great perfection, the absolute fruition of the qualities of enlightenment. Nevertheless, it is presented in a systematic order to allow disciples to begin to enter that state. The teachings are divided into three series; the *mind* series, the *space* series, and the *instruction* series, also known as the 'innermost essence'. Over the course of time, more and more attention has been given to the last of these. Two major lines of transmission of the innermost essence exist, one deriving from Vimalamitra and one deriving from Padmasambhava.

The basic ground of dzok chen is actually the true nature of reality, our fundamental nature. In this nature all phenomena, whether those of samsara or nirvana, have in fact been pure because empty of any essence from time without beginning. Thus, ultimately, there is no difference between a buddha and a sentient being. Within this primordial purity there is the uninterrupted manifestation of pure awareness, known in Tibetan as *rigpa*. The luminous power of awareness to manifest appearances is referred to as the spontaneously existent quality of the basic ground. That is the basis of dzok chen, the underlying reality of our being and of the entire universe.

We apprehend the underlying reality of the basis through the twin meditations of *trek-cho*, 'direct cutting', and *to-gal*, 'leap over'. However, before one can begin the practices of dzok chen, it is necessary to draw upon a series of preliminaries, known in Tibetan as the *ngondro*. They mature the disciple so that the subtle and profound teachings of dzok chen will work properly. We might be attracted to these profound teachings of dzok chen but just as with the higher tantric teachings of the other traditions, immature entry into them only causes spiritual chaos and conceit.

The preliminaries themselves are practised in two stages. First, an 'outer' section, drawing upon the teachings of the sutras and which comprises the following four-fold contemplation, often known as 'The Four Thoughts that Turn the Mind to Dharma'. Thus in sequence we should consider:

- *The preciousness and rarity of human birth –*
  the basis for dharma practice;

- *Impermanence and death – the encouragement to practise;*

- *Karma, cause and effect – discriminating between virtuous and non-virtuous actions;*

- *The defects of samsara – engendering renunciation.*

Secondly, the inner section drawing upon the sutras and tantras and which comprises the following five meditations:

- *Taking refuge – developing faith in the Three Jewels and the Three Roots (Lama, Yidam and Dakini);*

- *Developing bodhichitta – maintaining and strengthening one's bodhisattva vow;*

- *Meditation and recitation of Vajrasattva – purifying obscurations, breakage of vows and imprints of negative karma;*

- *Offering the mandala – accumulating merit and wisdom;*

- *Guru-yoga – receiving the blessings of the lama and lineage.*

Each of these 'inner' preliminaries has a key element which is accomplished one hundred thousand times, thus creating the necessary space for the practice to be effective.

In addition to the preliminaries, most Nyingma yogins utilize the development and fulfilment stage practices found in maha-yoga and anu-yoga respectively. Such practices further refine one's readiness to embark on dzok chen itself. Thus one might well rely upon one of the eight deities of maha-yoga, such as Vajrakilaya.

Once well established in these techniques we can proceed to the two meditations of dzok chen itself, known, as we have already noted, as trek-cho and to-gal.

Trek-cho begins when our vajrayana master introduces us to the fundamental purity of mind. For such a master to be capable of doing this, he needs to have realized dzok chen himself, for this introduction to mind is no mere textual teaching or philosophical instruction but a transmission of awareness itself. Once such an introduction has been effected, it is stabilized in meditation through remaining one with the expanse of awareness throughout experiences of both stillness and fluctuating thought. When this utter decisiveness is in place, trek-cho is brought to fruition by liberating whatever arises, thoughts, emotional disturbances and meditative experiences, into the naked stream of awareness, both in periods of contemplation and in everyday life. Thus, we cut through directly to the underlying purity of awareness, the inherent energy of the basic ground of reality. It said in the tradition that those who have mastered trek-cho are able to manifest the 'rainbow body' at the time of their death. In this state of realization all parts of the body disappear into emptiness, leaving behind only the hair and nails. Such an outer sign betokens the utter dissolution of ego. At this time rainbows appear in the sky to mark the yogin's passing. Even today one still hears of such apparently miraculous events occurring on the death of accomplished practitioners.

To-gal, meaning 'leap over', is the second aspect of dzok chen practice. By utilizing its extremely esoteric methods, we are able to apprehend and perfect the processes by which the luminosity of awareness radiates outwards as the appearances of the phenomenal world. One could compare it to the development stage of anuttara tantra, where one's vision is transformed when the whole world is visualized as a *mandala*, a magical palace, of the buddhas. However, in to-gal one does not visualize buddha realms but experiences them as an actual reality, since the very world itself, issuing as it does from one's luminous awareness, is naturally the mandala of the peaceful and wrathful deities. Those yogins who achieve mastery of to-gal obtain the luminous wisdom-body of a buddha, a state of perfection achieved in the past by such masters in the past as Padmasambhava and Vimalamitra.

The Schools of the New Tantras

At this point, we can turn to the three schools that follow the 'new' tantras, the form of vajrayana that was transmitted to Tibet from the eleventh century onwards. Two principal schools developed in that century, the Sakya and the Kagyu.

Sakya

The Sakya school actually began in the year of 1073 with the foundation of a meditation centre in the province of Tsang at a place called Sakya ('grey earth'). The centre was founded by a master called Konchog Gyalpo who hailed from the Khön clan, an influential, aristocratic family whose connection with Buddhism went back to the time of Guru Padmasambhava in the eighth century. The members of this family had been practitioners of the 'ancient' tantras since those times but in the mid-eleventh century Konchog Gyalpo and his brothers become convinced that many of the tantric practices of the ancient transmission had become compromised by the dubious behaviour of some of their adherents. Therefore, they looked to the new tantras that were being propagated in Tibet at that time by such figures as Drokmi Lotsawa whom Konchog Gyalpo sought out as his lama and from whom he received some teachings on the Hevajra tantra. It was following Konchog Gyalpo that the Sakya tradition really turned from being a small-scale grouping into one of the greatest schools that the Buddhist world has ever seen. This transformation is due largely to the work of the 'Five Great Masters'. This eminent series of spiritual masters of the twelfth and thirteenth centuries were all members of the Khön family, which has remained to this day the ruling dynasty of the Sakya school.

Kunga Nyingpo (1092–1158), Konchog Gyalpo's son, known as 'the Great Sakyapa', began the process of enriching the Sakya school with an immense variety of teachings, both philosophical and tantric, which he received from different masters such as the erudite translator Bari Lotsawa and Shangton Chobar.

Such was Sachen Kunga Nyingpo's fame that inevitably it attracted the jealousy of other religious teachers. As a result some particularly envious rivals dispatched a young man to assassinate him. The would-be-killer stole into the room at night where Kunga Nyingpo was sleeping. He pulled back the bedclothes intending to stab him, when to his amazement he saw that Sachen's body had become transformed into that of the Buddha Chenrezig, embodiment of universal compassion. Shocked, the now repentant attacker confessed his evil intention and begged to be accepted as the master's disciple.

81

Under **Sonam Tsemo** (1141–1182) and **Jetsun Drakpa Gyaltsen**, (1147–1216) two of Sachen Kunga Nyingpo's sons, the expansion of the school continued. Like their father, both were scholars and accomplished yogins who composed many texts on both sutra and tantra topics. Jetsun Drakpa Gyaltsen's mastery of vajrayana yoga was so great that it is said he was able to suspend his vajra (religious sceptre) and bell in mid-air and hang his robe over a rainbow.

Sakya Pandita Kunga Gyaltsen (1182–1251), the grandson of Kunga Nyingpo, and usually known simply as 'Sakya Pandita' ('the Sakya scholar'), was the fourth and perhaps greatest of the early Sakya masters. He is famed as the only Tibetan master to possess the outer signs and characteristics of a fully enlightened buddha. One could describe Sakya Pandita as a 'Renaissance Man', combining as he did spiritual accomplishment with an encyclopedic knowledge of both Buddhist learning and the secular arts and sciences taught in India, such as poetics, lexicography, music, logic and epistemology. Sakya Pandita introduced these disciplines to the Tibetan world, and for this, he earned a reputation among his followers and among all Tibetans as being the incarnation of Manjushri, the bodhisattva of wisdom. Even during his life time Sakya Pandita's fame was so extensive that philosophers of the Hindu Vedanta school came from India to debate with him. Sakya Pandita defeated each of them in turn through his mastery of logic and thus compelled them to convert to Buddhism.

Sakya Pandita, eminent master of the Sakya tradition

Chogyal Phakpa (1235–1280), nephew of Sakya Pandita, would ensure that more was to follow. He not only took up the mantle from Sakya Pandita of directing the Sakya school but became the lama of the world-famous Mongol Emperor, Kublai Khan, who had established control over the entire Chinese Empire. In return for his master's teachings, the Khan established the Sakya school as rulers of Tibet, a position which they held for the next 75 years. This was a time when the Sakya school stamped its genius upon Tibetan Buddhism.

Following the decline of its secular power, the Sakya school concentrated entirely upon spiritual matters, eventually giving rise to two great sub-sects; the Ngor, founded by Kunga Zangpo (1382–1457) and the Tshar, founded by Losal Gyamtso (1494–1556). Even in the nineteenth century the spiritual influence of the Sakya school was undiminished, playing as it did a major role in the ecumenical renaissance that took place in the Eastern Tibet.

The Path and Its Fruit

As we have indicated, the spiritual teachings of the Sakya school had an extraordinary reach, drawing upon all the different currents of Buddhism brought to Tibet from India. Among this vast quantity of teachings, undoubtedly the most significant for the Sakya school is the cycle known in Tibetan as *lam-dre*, 'The Path and its Fruit'. This is a cycle of teachings that originated in the mystical experience of the ninth-century Indian yogin, Virupa.

The lam-dre provides a systematic progression through the meditation practices of both the sutras and tantras. At its heart is the vision of reality known as 'the inseparability of samsara and nirvana'. This is both the philosophical doctrine underpinning the lam-dre and the ultimate realization of the yogin who practises these esoteric instructions. In this vision the apparently impure world, in which we live and have our being, is recognized as nothing other than nirvana itself. In the final analysis, since samsara, comprising the six realms of suffering, is devoid of intrinsic nature one need not reject it but instead recognize its emptiness as nirvana itself. As it says in the Hevajra tantra, 'By rejecting samsara one will never find nirvana.'

One can see this as an instance of the vajrayana view in which the only difference between buddhas and ordinary beings is that the latter do not recognize their own true nature. Due to this crucial distinction, sentient beings wander throughout the suffering of the cyclic existence. To attain nirvana, one only need recognize that it is already present within what appears to our presently deluded vision as samsara. To transform our perception and thus recognize the inseparability of samsara and nirvana we should practise the lam-dre system. The powerful techniques of the lam-dre particularly draw upon the practices of the Hevajra tantra. The development and completion stage yogas of Hevajra provide the necessary experiential framework for decisive insight into 'the inseparability of samsara and nirvana'.

Kagyu

Whilst the Sakya school is marked for its eminence in scholarship and tantric ritual, the Kagyu school is famed as the school of meditation and yogic practice. Indeed, one of its alternative names is 'the practice lineage'. Like the Sakya school, the Kagyu arose in the eleventh century, at the time of a renewed thirst in Tibet for authentic teachings. The founding patriarchs of the Kagyu school were Marpa 'the translator', Milarepa, the great ascetic yogin and poet,

and the incomparable Gampopa, monk, scholar, and foremost sys-
tematizer of the Kagyu school.

Marpa (1012–1097) spent approximately twenty years in India
over the course of three separate expeditions from Tibet. From
renowned and accomplished masters such as Naropa and Maitripa,
he inherited a body of teachings that would form the core spiritual
syllabus for later generations of Kagyu practitioners in Tibet. The
crown jewels of this corpus of dharma were the teachings known as
mahamudra ('the Great Seal') and the 'Six Dharmas of Naropa', both
of which are actually part of anuttara tantra. The Six Dharmas of
Naropa comprise techniques for gaining control over the subtle
body of winds, channels and drops. Mahamudra is more concerned
with the actual direct experience of the nature of mind itself.

Although Marpa was a translator, scholar and tantric yogin, to all
outward appearances he lived the life of a wealthy farmer, married
to the Lady Dagmema, and father of several children. However, his
close disciples recognized him as a buddha in person. Marpa had
intended to transmit his spiritual authority to his older son but this
proved impossible and instead the lineage passed to his student, the
poet and yogin, Milarepa.

Milarepa, great yogin and poet of the Kagyu school

WAY of

Milarepa (1040–1123) is famed throughout the Tibetan world not just as a patriarch of the Kagyu but as one of the paramount examples of the diligence and courage needed on the spiritual path. Born in Gungthang in Southern Tibet, Milarepa had to rise above a deluge of difficulties and obstacles from his early life, to become Marpa's student at the age of 38. Endowed with total devotion to his master, Milarepa received the precious vajrayana instructions and then spent many years meditating upon them in the snowy mountains of Nepal and Tibet, clad only in a white cotton robe.

Unlike his guru who practised vajrayana in the midst of everyday life, Milarepa practised in great austerity and therefore did not take an ordinary human consort as his partner in vajrayana yoga. In this role he was served by the goddess Tashi Tseringma. Milarepa first met this goddess at Chubar Menlung when she manifested herself in wrathful form during his meditation, causing the earth to shake. A host of malevolent demons appeared before him, the most hideous of whom were five flesh-eating demonesses. The chief of these, Tseringma herself, was clashing the sun and moon as cymbals while Milarepa saw the forest being shaken, rocks tossed, the sky ablaze and the earth flooded with water. This first encounter was followed by others during which Milarepa was gradually able to subdue Tseringma through the power of his meditative realization that all appearances are simply the manifestation of one's own mind and thus gods and demons have no intrinsic reality.

Milarepa eventually attained the level of buddhahood in his very lifetime through almost superhuman effort and went on to transmit his realization to disciples, not only in the formal manner of initiations and instructions but also through the medium of poetic composition and song, thereby continuing a tradition begun by his mahamudra forefathers, such as Saraha and Maitripa in India. Consequently,

Milarepa has become an unceasing inspiration to countless generations of practitioners.

Gampopa (1079–1173) was the chief student of Milarepa and the one to whom the latter entrusted the teachings received from Marpa. Gampopa had already had been through a number of years of spiritual training, which had taken place in the Kadam school. So when Gampopa became Milarepa's student, he brought with him all the discipline and precision of a monastic background.

On the occasion of Gampopa's first meeting with his master he presented him with an offering of gold and tea. Milarepa responded by insisting that Gampopa drink a human skullcup full of beer. Gampopa was reluctant to do this because it was an infringement of his monastic rules. However, he put aside his misgivings and drank the beer. Such confidence in his guru's instructions proved him to be a worthy recipient of Milarepa's teachings.

When he later became head of the fledgling Kagyu community in the southern part of Central Tibet, Gampopa synthesized the graduated, non-tantric path of the Kadam school with the tantric teachings of Milarepa. He also introduced monasticism. From the time of Gampopa onwards, especially in the two generations that followed, the Kagyu sect spread like wildfire through Tibet. Due to Gampopa's influence, it was primarily a monastic tradition, though not excluding a certain number of lay yogins.

This rapid period of growth was not without its difficulties. The Kagyu quickly splintered into numerous sub-sects, the 'four great' and 'eight minor' schools headed by Gampopa's chief disciples and their followers. Significant among these schools was the Karma Kagyu sub-sect, one of whose most important contributions to

89

WAY of

Tibetan Buddhism has been the custom of recognizing reincarnated lamas. This practice began in the thirteenth century with the discovery of Karma Pakshi, the reincarnation of Karmapa Dusum Chenpa (1110–1193), who had established the Karma Kagyu subsect. The seventeen successive incarnations of the Karmapa lama have headed the Karma Kagyu school to this present day, aided by other great incarnations such as the Shamar and Tai Situ lamas.

The Great Seal

It was mahamudra, the teaching inherited from Marpa's two Indian masters Naropa and Maitripa, that became the key meditation cycle of all the Kagyu schools in Tibet. The term 'mahamudra' itself, meaning 'Great Seal', signifies for the Kagyu tradition the manner in which the enlightened yogin 'seals' everything that arises within his field of experience with his understanding of emptiness. The whole phenomenal world is nothing other than mind and yet mind itself has no essence by which it can be grasped. It is as boundless as space itself, without centre or periphery, without origination or cessation. So whilst it may be said that all phenomena arise from mind, ultimately neither phenomena nor mind have any intrinsic nature but are like labels on space. Mind and the phenomenal world are therefore inseparable and empty. This unity cannot be reduced to anything fixed but is fluid, all-embracing and eternal. Such is the mahamudra view presented both by the great siddhas such as Tilopa, Naropa, Shabaripa and Maitripa and in Tibet by Marpa and Milarepa.

From the time of Gampopa onwards mahamudra was systematized into a graded series of practices. This sequence begins with the accomplishment of the outer and inner preliminaries comprising 'The Four Thoughts' plus taking refuge, bodhichitta, Vajrasattva, mandala offering and guru yoga already familiar to us from our account of the Nyingma tradition. Following the preliminaries the mahamudra practitioner is instructed in *shamatha*, 'calm abiding', which is understood here as uncontrived naturalness, the effortless relaxation of the mind into its natural state. As such it is not to be achieved by suspension of thought, subtle meditation techniques or any artificial means whatsoever. Alongside the training in shamatha it has become customary in the Kagyu tradition to prac-tise the meditation on the goddess Vajravarahi as the development stage and then the yogas of the Six Dharmas of Naropa as the com-pletion stage. This latter cycle consists of the yogas of heat, lumi-nosity, illusory body, dream, transference of consciousness and the intermediate state (bardo). These skilful methods refine one's con-sciousness and so allow the genuine stability of shamatha to arise more easily.

When the effortless spaciousness of shamatha has become a stable feature of one's experience, both in meditation sessions and in everyday life, one can begin the meditations of *vipashyana*, devel-oping insight into the nature of mind. At this point one receives 'direct introduction to the nature of mind' from one's lama, who of course must be a realized master of mahamudra for his introduction to be effective. It can be effected through words, symbols or even direct mind-to-mind transmission. It is said that just as the sun shines forth in all its splendour, when the clouds have disappeared from the sky so likewise buddha nature, concealed within the mind itself, needs only to be revealed through the master's instructions for it to manifest in all its brilliance. At this point thoughts and emo-tions, considered by ordinary meditators as obstacles in need of removal, are recognized as nothing but the manifestation of the true nature of mind, just as the rays of the sun are the manifestations of the sun's energy. Whatever arises from our mind, since our mind is

91

the dharmakaya, the ultimate reality of all buddhas, is simply the manifestation of the dharmakaya itself. This is the quintessence of mahamudra. As Saraha said, 'I looked in all ten directions, but whatever I saw, was this', and as Naropa said, 'I searched everywhere for the Buddha but finally found he dwelt within my own mind.'

Gelug

Finally, we come to the last of the four Tibetan schools, the Gelug. Though like the Kagyu and Sakya it belongs to the group of the new tantra schools, its foundations are actually somewhat later, being established in the late-fourteenth and early-fifteenth centuries. By that time, the transmission of Buddhism from India to Tibet had long ceased and Buddhism was fully Tibetan. This situation is reflected in the fact that the school's founder, Tsongkhapa from Amdo (1367–1419), in north-eastern Tibet, did not have to travel to India but rather was able to inherit the teachings and practices for his new tradition from Tibetan masters of other schools.

In many ways Tsongkhapa was a synthesizer of the philosophical and meditative teachings of other schools. He wove together textual lineages and tantric material from various traditions to provide the Gelug with its body of teachings. These included Sakya philosophical works and meditation practices from the Sakya, Kagyu and various other smaller schools. Most importantly, he drew upon the approach of Atisha and the Kadam school. Tsongkhapa's strong emphasis on the 'graduated path' made the Gelug resemble the early Kadam so much that his followers became known as the 'New Kadam'. The innovatory side of Tsongkhapa can be seen in his philosophical teachings, where he developed an idiosyncratic version of madhyamaka, that attracted some criticism from other philosophers, most notably Sonam Seng-ge of the Sakya school. Another important element in the Gelug curriculum was the study of logic and epistemology, to which Tsongkhapa gave more emphasis than had earlier Tibetan masters. Tsongkhapa was perhaps most notable for his insistence upon strict observance of the rules of monastic discipline as set forth in the vinaya. This last fact led to his school eventually being dubbed the Gelug (the Virtuous Way).

During Tsongkhapa's lifetime many disciples collected around him, so many in fact that they were able to establish the monastery of Ganden, some 35 miles from Lhasa. Shortly after that, two other major monasteries, Sera and Drepung, were founded. Over the next two centuries, the school built up a very substantial membership and strong support throughout Tibet. In 1642, a high-ranking master of the school, the fifth Dalai Lama, Ngawang Losang Gyamtso (1617–1682), was put on the throne of Tibet by Mongol intervention. This made the Gelug school effectively the state church throughout much of Tibet, certainly throughout U-Tsang and Ngari, the central and western provinces of Tibet.

FIVE

TIBETAN BUDDHISM
In The West

Thirty years ago, Tibetan Buddhism was virtually unknown in the West. Now we find groups spread from Vladivostok to Buenos Aires. In this chapter, we consider how this has happened and what is the present situation of the four schools of Tibetan Buddhism. There is also finally a little speculation about the future.

Why has Tibetan Buddhism become so popular in the West? To answer this question, we have to go back into the mists of time, as least as far as the nineteenth century. However bizarre it now seems, Western interest in Tibetan Buddhism was first stimulated by the remarkable Madame Helena Petrovna Blavatsky, founder of the Theosophical Society. With her tales of 'mahatmas', discarnate entities and various other spectral phenomena, she popularized the notion of Tibet as a land of endless phantasmagoric wonders. In many ways her most important successor in this line of mystical hokum was Cyril Hoskins, known to a world-wide audience as 'Lobsang Rampa'. Out of a mixture of Madame Blavatsky's theosophical jiggery-pokery and an intensive reading of Alexandra David-Neel's highly-coloured accounts of her Tibetan travels, Lobsang Rampa created a picture of Tibet which entranced millions of Westerners in the late 1950s and early 1960s. In the fetid imagination of that author Tibet was a land in which enlightenment was obtained through the drilling of a small aperture in the front of the skull. (Do not try this at home, children!)

The fascination with Tibet that the Blavatsky/Rampa lineage created has left behind a legacy of misunderstanding and, in particular, a tendency for overheated imagination concerning the powers and role of Tibetan lamas. Even when we turn from such lurid accounts of Tibetan Buddhism to the view propagated throughout more respectable Buddhist circles in the West, we see that Tibetan Buddhism was actually often regarded as in some ways not wholly Buddhist. For many years Theravada and Zen were portrayed as more acceptable forms of Buddhism. Both were seen as rational, modern and scientific in a way that Tibetan Buddhism could never be.

What changed all this? Misconceptions about Tibetan Buddhism were largely overcome as a result of the tragic events of 1959, when Tibetan resistance to Chinese communist occupation was finally crushed. In the resulting diaspora, up to 100,000 Tibetan refugees fled to India, led by H.H. the Dalai Lama. Ironically, it was this tragedy which actually precipitated the transmission of Tibetan Buddhism to the West.

In the 1960s, the first task of Tibetans in exile was the reconstitution of their own culture and religion in the refugee settlements of India and Nepal. Thus at that time, serious involvement in Tibetan Buddhism was extremely small-scale. That began to change in the 1970s when, perhaps spurred on by the cultural changes occurring in the West, it spread to Europe and North America and a more youthful audience for Buddhism was created. This new audience was one that was fully prepared to engage with the power of Tibetan Buddhism.

Gelug

Let us look at the four schools of Tibetan Buddhism and the impact they have made on the West. It seems most appropriate to begin with the Gelug because in our consideration of the four schools in Tibet we ended with this school, noting that it effectively became the established church of Tibetan Buddhism in the last 300 years. One could expect, therefore, that it would be one

97

of the more powerful forms of Buddhism in the West. The fortunes of Gelug in the West are largely inextricable from the activity of H.H. the Dalai Lama. Naturally, His Holiness has remained the rallying-point for Tibetans inside and outside of Tibet in exile. Incidentally, one point that is often misunderstood by Westerners is the Dalai Lama's status within the Gelug school. The Dalai Lama, who, in a succession of incarnations since 1642 has been king of Tibet, is not actually the head of the Gelug school. The role of head is an elected post that belongs to the senior abbot of Ganden, the first Gelug monastery, which was founded by Tsongkhapa himself. This fact, of course, does not gainsay the tremendous influence H.H. the Dalai Lama has on the Gelug tradition and even on Buddhism as a whole in Tibet. One might even say that the Dalai Lama has now become the leading figure of Buddhism in the world, a status signified not least by his receipt of the Nobel Peace Prize and many world tours, which have brought him increasing renown and respect from people of all religious traditions and none.

Inevitably, the massive presence of the Dalai Lama has, despite his own non-sectarian leanings, created a lot of Western interest in the Gelug school. One particular location that has stimulated this interest in the Gelug tradition over the last three decades has been the hill-station of Dharamsala in Northern India where His Holiness resides. There, at the Library of Tibetan Works and Archives as well as in some of the monastic institutions and groups around Dharamsala, many Westerners, young and not so young, have had their first encounter with Tibetan Buddhism through the excellent programmes provided for them.

Of all the representatives of the Gelug tradition who have gained Western adherents, the most active have been Lama Thubten Yeshe and his disciple Thubten Zopa Rinpoche who, in 1975, founded the

Federation for Preservation of the Mahayana Tradition (FPMT). These two tireless workers for Buddhism first attracted Western disciples at the end of the 1960s when they were resident near Kathmandu in Nepal. They went on to run annual courses for Westerners in Kopan some miles outside the city. This in turn triggered the setting up of the FPMT, which has acted as an umbrella organization for their many centres scattered throughout the western world. Those centres are now under the spiritual authority of Zopa Rinpoche, Lama Yeshe having died in 1983. Very large study centres belonging to the FPMT exist now in America, Australia, New Zealand, England, France, Spain and elsewhere. The teaching style of Zopa Rinpoche and Lama Yeshe is grounded in the Gelug spiritual syllabus, perhaps most strongly emphasizing the lam-rim or 'graduated path', taught originally by Tsongkhapa. Thus, to a certain extent, they reserve the most academic aspects of the Gelug sect only for those judged sufficiently mature and committed in their studies. As one might expect, there has been a strong emphasis on monasticism within this organization. Although Lama Yeshe adopted a rather Western mode of discourse in order to convey his teachings, the FPMT remains identifiable as a traditional Gelug organization, albeit perhaps of a more populist kind than one might encounter in the large monasteries of India that are now beginning to admit serious Western students.

It is impossible at the moment to make any reliable evaluation of the number of Westerners following the Gelug, or in fact any of the four Tibetan traditions. However, it would be a fairly well supported guess if one were to suggest that it is the Gelug and Kagyu traditions that have so far proved most popular in western countries.

One other group which has sprung fully formed from the Gelug tradition and been exceedingly vigorous in recent years is the

99

organization that somewhat anachronistically calls itself the 'New Kadampa' tradition. The organization was founded by Geshe Kalzang Gyamtso, a graduate of Sera Monastic University. He first came to the West in the employ of Lama Yeshe and Zopa Rinpoche as one of the teachers appointed to their large institute in the United Kingdom. However, in subsequent years, Geshe Kalzang managed to attract a number of his employers' erstwhile disciples to himself and at the beginning of the 1990s he effectively seceded from the Gelug tradition. However, his organization should at least in part be understood as representing the party of hard-line Gelug opposition to the non-sectarian policies of H.H. the Dalai Lama.

Thanks largely to astute publicity and considerable financial acumen the New Kadam has proved extremely successful in the West. It has a large and very evangelical following, particularly among young people who are as remarkable for their fervour as for their lack of curiosity about other forms of Buddhism and indeed their own community's antecedents.

Sakya

The Sakya tradition is often described nowadays as the smallest of the four schools and has perhaps been the slowest to spread in the West. The most influential figure of the Sakya school has undoubtedly been the 41st patriarch H.H. Sakya Trizin, who has directed the reconstruction of the tradition from exile in India and the West. His Holiness was born in 1945 in Southern Tibet. When he came to India in 1959 as head of the tradition, he was still a young teenager. Yet, with his innate spiritual accomplishment and brilliance, he has proven an extremely effective leader of the

Sakya tradition. Through his many visits to the West, he has more than ensured that the tradition has a following in North America and Europe.

Other members of the Khön family, the ruling dynasty of the tradition, have participated in this work. Of particular note in this respect, His Holiness' sister, Jetsun Chime Luding, though married and a mother of five children, has worked untiringly from her base in Vancouver for the tradition. Likewise, His Eminence Dagchen Rinpoche, a member of another branch of the Khön dynasty, has worked for many years in the United States for the Sakya school. In Europe, centres have been established in many countries, such as France by Phende Rinpoche and the United Kingdom by Karma Thinley Rinpoche, grand master of the Dechen Community. Through these various lamas and centres in North America and Europe, the Sakya tradition has carried on with its distinctive approach, combining scholarship and meditation and supported by the reconstitution of the Sakya monasteries in India.

Kagyu

The Kagyu school, along with the Gelug, has perhaps played the dominant role in the propagation of Tibetan Buddhism in the West. It should be noted from the outset that though various sub-sects of the Kagyu have come to the West, by far the most influential among these has been the Karma Kagyu. This sub-sect has traditionally been headed by successive incarnations of the highly revered lama, H.H. the Gyalwa Karmapa. The sixteenth Karmapa, Rangjung Rigpai Dorje, was able to make three major visits to the West before his untimely passing away in Chicago in 1981.

Among the Kagyu lamas to have come to the West, perhaps the two most influential were the rather interestingly different characters of Chogyam Trungpa Rinpoche (1939–87) and Kalu Rinpoche (1904–91). In terms of the number of centres established and the followers they have attracted, they were certainly the most successful. Trungpa Rinpoche, who came out of Tibet in 1959, was considered by many one of the most gifted interpreters of Tibetan Buddhism for the Western world. His dharma work commenced in Great Britain in the mid-1960s when he established Samye Ling, a meditation centre in Scotland, along with his disciple and friend Akong Rinpoche. After a rather messy falling out with Akong Rinpoche, Trungpa moved to the United States where he established the Vajradhatu association of meditation centres. It was perhaps Trungpa's literary style, as well as his lifestyle, which was rather unconventional for a Tibetan lama, that attracted many people to him in the States. Not least of these was a significant contingent of writers from the beat generation led by Allen Ginsberg. Such disciples certainly attracted a wide hearing for Trungpa Rinpoche's restyling of Kagyu dharma for a highly secularized American audience. Eventually, and to the surprise of his early American disciples, Trungpa Rinpoche transformed Vajradhatu into an organization that strove to reproduce the formal culture of an oriental court modelled on the mythical realm of Shambhala, with Trungpa Rinpoche himself as the monarch. Although he succumbed to an untimely death in 1987, it would be fair to describe Trungpa Rinpoche as the most important figure in the first wave of Tibetan Buddhism in America. Vajradhatu has since, after negotiating a series of difficulties, passed into the hands of one of Trungpa Rinpoche's own sons, Osel Mukpo.

The other major figure in the propagation of Kagyu Buddhism in the West in the last two decades, Kalu Rinpoche, a master of both the Karma and Shangpa Kagyu traditions, had gained in Tibet a great reputation for the austerity of his practice and his considerable accomplishment as a yogin. He was charged by H.H. Karmapa with the task of spreading traditional Karma Kagyu Buddhism in the West from 1972 onwards and adopted a very orthodox Kagyu style, emphasizing meditation on Chenrezi, the deity of compassion. Kalu Rinpoche also established a number of three-year retreat centres in the West. This approach attracted those who were perhaps more sympathetic to traditional forms of Kagyu Buddhism than those people who flocked to Trungpa Rinpoche. With one exception, his French disciple Lama Denis Dondrup, Kalu Rinpoche did not appoint his Western disciples as teachers. He left behind a younger generation of Tibetan and Bhutanese monks to supervise his numerous centres.

The rapid progress of Karma Kagyu Buddhism in the West has to some extent been thrown into question by the continuing controversy about the seventeenth reincarnation of the Karmapa. Two parties, one centred around Shamar Rinpoche (*b.* 1952) and the other around Situ Rinpoche (*b.* 1954), have advanced competing candidates as the authentic reincarnation of the head of the Karma Kagyu tradition. This may seem a rather remote disagreement for most Westerners, even among those who have something of an interest in Buddhism. However, since the authority of the lama and the inviolability of the lineage is of such paramount importance in Tibetan Buddhism, this issue is a very live and pressing problem for those seriously committed to the Karma Kagyu school, even in the West.

Nyingma

Like the Sakya school, the Nyingma has made a quieter impact in the West than the bigger Kagyu and Gelug schools. Again, as with the Sakya, it has been the high lamas of the school who have had the greatest influence. In this case, undoubtedly the two main figures have been Dingo Khyentse Rinpoche (1910–91) and Dudjom Rinpoche (1904–87). They not only attracted Westerners visiting India as disciples but also made a number of visits to the West, even establishing centres in such unlikely places as the Dordogne region of France. Both these paramount lamas of the Nyingma tradition strove to train their close Western disciples in the traditional manner and practices of the Nyingma tradition, primarily through bestowing initiations and teachings for accomplishment in retreat.

The tradition has not been without its more popularizing figures and in this connection one should certainly mention Tarthang Tulku (*b.* 1935). He has perhaps gone the furthest in his attempt to recast Tibetan Buddhism in a form more acceptable to the modern world, or at least the Californian part of it. In this respect, Tarthang Tulku has been followed by his younger contemporary, Sogyal Rinpoche (*b.* 1946). As a child, he spent some years with the great rimé master Jamyang Khyentse Chokyi Lodro, and later enjoyed several years of education Western-style in India before a rather brief sojourn at Cambridge University. Sogyal Rinpoche's undoubted familiarity with many features of Western life has made him one of the most successful Tibetan figures on the present scene.

So what is the overall situation facing Tibetan Buddhism in the West? Tibetan Buddhism is almost unique among religious traditions in the world in its very distance from the assumptions of late-20th/early-21st century culture. Perhaps that is why it might have seemed so unlikely to achieve the degree of success that it has done in the West. However, one must hope that Tibetan Buddhism can remain true to its essential principles at a time when there are some Westerners and not a few Tibetans who appear determined to dilute its purity in order to benefit from its current status as a valuable commodity in the spiritual supermarket.

It must be conceded, however, that it will perhaps cease to be termed 'Tibetan Buddhism' and instead may simply be understood as vajrayana Buddhism of the Kagyu, Sakya, Nyingma and Gelug schools in the West. In this way it would then continue to be the authentic vajrayana, albeit now with centres and followers in the West that are just as important as any of those in Tibet or among the exiled Tibetan community. Perhaps one significant pointer in this direction is the fact that a number of Tibetan masters have actually authorized some of their Western disciples as lamas in their own right.

In the final analysis, we should be optimistic about the future of Tibetan Buddhism, because the Buddha taught us that all men and women, and indeed all sentient beings have buddha nature. This nature does not belong to any one culture. It does not even belong to Tibetans, great though their contribution has been to the preservation of Buddhism. Even in our world with its preoccupation with politics, its agitation and its complexity, the message of the Buddha that all men and women possess this heart of goodness is just as relevant as ever. The teachings preserved for so long by the Tibetan sages are now equally at home right here in the concrete and open fields of the West as they were in the highlands of Tibet. The lineage of wisdom and compassion continues.

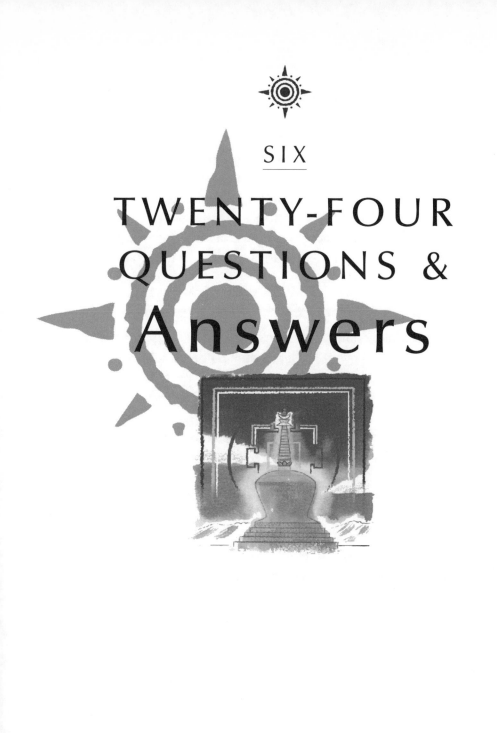

SIX

TWENTY-FOUR QUESTIONS & Answers

1. What is enlightenment?

One way to answer this question is to look at the etymology of the Tibetan term for 'Buddha'. When the Tibetans came to translate Buddhist scriptures from the original Sanskrit, they focused very closely on the meaning behind the terminology rather than the literal value of the words. This includes the word for Buddha itself, the title of our teacher. In Sanskrit, Buddha means the 'Awakened One', indicating he has awakened to the true nature of reality.

The Tibetans translated 'buddha' as 'sang-gye', which is formed through the conjunction of two terms. The first, 'sang', means 'to have purified or removed'. This indicates that a buddha has purified or removed all the elements that cover the true nature of one's mind, that is to say the age-old habits of ignorance, desire, hatred and other mental poisons. A buddha is therefore someone who has freed himself or herself from the constraints and blindness of those states of mind. The second part of the word, 'gye', has the sense of 'expanding'. Once one has cleared away the obscurations or veils covering one's own true nature, the innate qualities of wisdom and compassion blossom and expand.

Enlightenment is, therefore, to be partly understood in a negative sense as the clearing away of all that is foreign to our fundamental qualities, or buddha nature, but it is also the revelation of the intrinsically positive qualities of wisdom, compassion and power through which we can work endlessly for all beings. To become enlightened, then, means firstly to free ourselves from the hindrances of an egotistical view of the world and secondly, having freed ourselves, to engage in the world for the benefit of all beings.

2. How long does it take to become enlightened?

There is no set time. The qualities of wisdom and compassion that we uncover on the path exist within all of us right now. One can even say they are our primordial nature. What we are trying to do on the path is to free ourselves from identifying with that which is false, such as the notion that our body is our self, or that our distorted thoughts and emotions are our self. How long that will take us depends upon how much effort we put into following the spiritual path, but enlightenment is in a sense available to us right now.

Of course, one needs to find an effective method for removing the obscurations. Having found the skilful teachers who can impart these to us, we then need to be fully committed to using them. It is said that there are beings, like the dzok chen master Garab Dorje, for whom enlightenment follows instantaneously upon their hearing one line of the teaching. However, such beings are as rare as stars seen in the daytime. The vast majority of us need to follow a graduated and systematic path. However, if we follow the most powerful of Buddha's teachings, the vajrayana, then it is possible to become enlightened in this very life. Even if that is not possible, by sincerely setting out on the spiritual path in this life we should be confident that in successive lives we will carry on with this upward movement towards enlightenment.

3. Does Tibetan Buddhism have any connection with the New Age movement?

I recognize that there are many sincere people involved in what are nowadays called 'New Age' movements. From a Buddhist point of view, however, it is definitely unhelpful to construct a school or movement that cannibalizes elements of different and even contradictory religions or teachings, attempting to create some kind of synthesis from them. We need to be discriminatory in our spiritual endeavours.

We need to be clear-headed and informed about the real nature of the Buddhist tradition. This only comes about through study and contemplation over a long period of time. Study begins for most people with the reading of introductory books on Buddhism available in bookshops and libraries. Yet, in doing so, we must exercise care to ensure that those books are actually written by representatives of authentic traditions of Buddhism, because nobody else has the authority, or indeed the ability, to convey Buddha's teachings. When we move beyond that initial period of reading and reflection, we can enter into an apprenticeship with authentic masters of these traditions. This is how we ensure that we will receive only teachings that have come from immaculate sources.

One quite common way of distinguishing between Buddhism and New Age movements is to examine the nature of the teachings. The Buddha's teachings are very often radical and challenging to our sense of ego, to our prejudices and even to our preconceptions and assumptions about what a spiritual tradition should be. They are directed at the elimination of all self-centredness. It is sadly all too often the case that much New Age spirituality is in fact dedicated to the exact opposite, the reinforcement of the obsession with self, which according to Buddha is the root of all our suffering. So it is here that we can often see the clearest evidence of the distinction between Buddhist and New Age teachings.

Another diversion from Buddhism is seen in the way that many people who are interested in spirituality, and thus attracted to New

Age movements, unthinkingly accept most contemporary Western values as being in harmony with spirituality. Yet, much of Buddha's teaching, particularly his ethical teaching, is in direct contradiction to modern Western values. The challenge that the traditional teaching poses to modern moral assumptions on matters such as abortion should alert us to the distinctiveness of Buddhism. When a movement, however much it attempts to pass itself off as incorporating Buddhist values, is totally consistent with modern liberal humanist assumptions, then it is more likely than not to be New Age and nothing to do with traditional Buddhism.

4. How can we choose a book about meditation?

Actually, in a way you cannot choose a book in the hope of learning everything about meditation, because it is said in the Buddhist tradition that for such things we need the guidance of teachers, those who have already gone down the spiritual path. They are learned in the variety of teachings and will, even more importantly, have some experiences of the territory that we must pass through on the spiritual path. In particular, they will understand how to deal with the different types of meditation experiences that occur and the different types of pitfalls and problems that crop up. These are things we simply cannot learn from a book.

If somebody were looking for a book on meditation and he or she knew that they were not interested in Buddhism, then it should be said that this book or any other on Buddhism is not appropriate for them. Buddhism is a spiritual system that has the all-encompassing aim of discovering our true nature and awakening the qualities of wisdom and compassion to benefit all sentient beings. By contrast, many people who are interested in meditation nowadays are interested solely in gaining relief from stress and other contemporary problems. There is nothing wrong with such aims of course but they are not comparable to the far more profound and vast aims of Buddhism.

If somebody were looking for a book on Buddhism, I would advise that they start with something very simple such as the basic teachings on how we can choose between skilful forms of action that lead to happiness and unskilful forms of action that lead to suffering. We need books that explain those points so that, even before meeting any teachers, we feel that we can make a difference to our lives by following Buddha's very simple and helpful advice. Once we have read about those teachings and seen their usefulness in bringing about a more relaxed and kind approach to people and things in our life, we will have the confidence to go deeper into the teachings. Start with something very simple, taken from any one of the Buddhist traditions, whether Theravada, Chinese, Japanese or Tibetan Buddhism; it does not really matter which one. Then you will at least know that it has not been mixed up with all kinds of unexamined Western assumptions.

5. When we take refuge in the Three Jewels, does it mean that we take refuge in all Buddhist traditions?

Yes it does, because no matter how we divide the different teachings of Buddhism, whether in terms of their nature: hinayana or mahayana; or in terms of their origin: Southeast Asian, Tibetan, Chinese, or Japanese; all forms of Buddhism start from a common root, which is the teaching given by Buddha himself. No matter what kind of Buddhism we follow, the three basic principles in which we must place our trust and confidence are the Three Jewels. As explained earlier, these are the Buddha, the great teacher who showed us the way to liberation, the dharma, the teachings he gave us explaining how we can follow the path to freedom, and the sangha, the men and women who have gone before us on the spiritual path and can help us with the practice of the dharma. When you take refuge and thereby formally become a Buddhist, you are not enclosing yourself within a single tradition. Taking refuge in the Three Jewels makes you a follower of Buddha himself. That is a really important point and one that we need to understand in order that we do not fall into the narrowness of assuming that one particular Buddhist tradition is better than the rest. All the Buddhist traditions that exist in the world have come from Buddha's original teachings and all are equally valuable. Even though it is necessary to study and practise one tradition primarily, the very fact that the act of taking refuge is common to all of these different traditions means that one should nonetheless feel part of the greater sangha, the sangha of all Buddhists. This will give our practice the necessary width and openness that are so essential for true spiritual growth, which is never anything to do with partiality, bigotry or feelings of superiority.

6. Nowadays some people regard themselves as Buddhist but at the same time think that it is good to practise Christianity or another religion at the same time. Is this possible?

I am afraid that when people attempt to do this, they are actually ignoring a very basic Buddhist teaching. There are three different trainings we should follow in order to maintain and strengthen the sense of connection we develop with the Three Jewels in taking refuge (see chapter 2). Having taken refuge in the Buddha, we should not take refuge in other teachers or gods. The reason for this is that taking refuge in the Buddha means to see him as the supremely skilful teacher, the one who has clearly discriminated the true nature of phenomena and the one who is able to lead us out of the cycle of suffering. Relating to the Buddha in this way implies that we regard his wisdom as unequalled by other religious teachers and figures. We cannot honestly say we are following Buddha, with his particular explanation of the nature of the universe, and simultaneously follow a teacher who has, for instance, a theistic vision of the universe, a view contradictory to the Buddha's non-theistic vision. By attempting to follow two ultimately contradictory systems, we will be split in half.

Having said that, there is of course much to admire in non-Buddhist religious systems. For instance, in some of the moral teachings and social services of modern religions we find a great deal of virtuous behaviour. We should appreciate those characteristics and praise them.

When we have made the decision, based upon intelligent understanding of Buddha's teachings, to practise Buddhism, we cannot then contradict the fundamental teachings by attempting to rely upon other religious systems. In this way, we uphold the distinctiveness of Buddhism, the very thing that attracted us to it in the first place, but we also show kindness and tolerance to the followers of other religious traditions.

7. If dzog chen and mahamudra are the highest teachings, allowing one to attain liberation immediately, why do we need to practise a graduated path?

Although a beginner can obtain a glimpse of the true nature of mind when he hears such teachings as dzog chen and mahamudra, it is an unfortunate fact that habitual distorted perception quickly causes the re-emergence of desire, hatred and ignorance. Such habits are so strong that even if we have some glimpse into our true nature, they quickly reassert themselves and cover over that glimpse. This means that the vast majority of us need a way of subduing these habits which obscure the true nature of mind. The initial way of dealing with them is to rely on such teachings as the 'Four Thoughts that turn the mind to dharma', generating bodhichitta and other methods of the hinayana and mahayana. A more powerful way of working with them, however, is to use the vajrayana methods. The obscuring habits themselves are frozen mental energy and vajrayana meditations of the development and fulfilment stages melt that frozen mental energy. When this energy is unlocked in this way, it is found to be nothing other than the buddha nature mind itself.

At this point one might ask if one could not simply practise the vajrayana and forego the more fundamental practices mentioned above? Unfortunately, I am afraid that for most people it is too difficult to use the vajrayana without first going through the basic teachings. Fundamental teachings such as the Four Thoughts are easily applicable to our present human situation. They allow us to develop a sane and steady approach to the spiritual path that will serve us well when we enter into the intensely powerful vajrayana. Without that sane and steady basis, we are likely to be swept off our feet by the deeper teachings. They are extremely powerful and their power may be misapplied and actually harm us. That is why in all the traditions: Kagyu, Sakya, Nyingma and Gelug, one begins with the Four Thoughts as the foundation for the tantric path.

8. The vajrayana method involves meditation on oneself as a buddha deity. How does this practice work exactly? It seems somewhat unnatural to pretend that you are something other than yourself, like a god with four arms, for instance.

Of course it is deeply unnatural to pretend that you are something you are not. In fact, one could say that this is the main cause of our problems. From beginningless time, we have been pretending that we are unchanging and immutable when we are not. At various times we imagine our self is our body, emotions or intellect, and that very delusion is what has landed us in the terrible mess we now experience. If that were what vajrayana was prescribing, it would not be an effective remedy to our problems in the slightest. So we should be clear about this. When the four classes of tantra in the vajrayana refer to deities upon which we meditate, they are not talking about external beings, like the kind familiar to us from theistic traditions. Nor are they talking about new personalities that we might somehow create within our mind. The deities are actually the embodiments of the primordially existent qualities that are already present within our awareness. Our awareness, in its true nature, is absolutely boundless, clear and compassionate. The deities themselves are to be understood as the manifestation of those intrinsic qualities. So when we meditate on our identity with those deities, we are actually unlocking and identifying with the deepest qualities of our fundamental nature.

9. In dharma it is said we must develop love and compassion. How then can you explain the presence of wrathful deities and destructive rituals in vajrayana? Is it not unkind to harm a sentient being?

We cannot imagine that Buddha would teach methods that would bring about suffering. Let us clarify, therefore, what we mean when we talk about wrathful deities. As I have already said, the deities taught in the four classes of tantra are neither external beings nor independent personalities. They are just the embodiment of our primordially enlightened nature whether they are in peaceful or wrathful form.

With regard to the so-called 'destructive' rituals which rely on either wrathful yidams or on the invocation of the 'dharma protectors', such as Mahakala and Mahakali, what is being represented here is a particular type of compassionate means for benefiting others. It is a fact that although most of the time we can benefit and give help to others through very gentle methods, sometimes we have to be more forceful. Just as in order to protect our children from harm we have to sometimes intervene vigorously, perhaps warning them with loud voices of some imminent danger, or snatching them away from a precipice, so the buddhas have to show wrathful forms in order to train those beings who are not able to respond to a more gentle approach in some particular situation. However, the underlying intention that is found in the wrathful rituals of the dharma protectors is one of the greatest love and compassion.

10. How do we choose a yidam?

In the tantric system the term 'yidam' refers primarily to the deity upon which we meditate. It should be pointed out that it is not always entirely a matter of us choosing yidams. Sometimes, particularly in the earlier part of our dharma career, we are more likely to simply practise the deities suggested to us by our masters. They will often prescribe whichever deities are regarded as most important in their tradition. Each of the four traditions preserves particular meditation systems associated with particular deities, although there is a great deal of commonality. For instance, across the four traditions it is usually the case that the beginners in vajrayana will practise deities such as Chenrezi, Tara and Manjushri. These deities are easily approachable and the qualities they embody, such as compassion and wisdom, are very useful for us in starting out on the vajrayana path. Then, if we fully go through the systematic yogic training of whichever one of the four schools we are following, it is

117

likely that we will eventually spend at least some time meditating on the deities that are particularly emphasized in that tradition, for instance Vajrayogini and Hevajra in Sakya or Vajrakilaya in Nyingma.

Choosing a yidam is usually something that evolves over a long period of time. When we have meditated on quite a few different deities over the course of our dharma practice, we will gradually develop a connection with a particular deity. That occurs when a certain deity is related to our deepest spiritual needs, the way in which we are best able to relate to ultimate reality. One need not worry, therefore, about which yidam to practise. Follow whatever your teacher suggests and gradually your affinity with a particular deity will reveal itself. It may be after two or three years; it may be after twenty. There is no particular time scale involved.

11. Is there a rule that men practise male yidams and women practise female?

There is no rule regarding this. Many men meditate upon the female deities Tara and Vajrayogini, and many women meditate upon male deities. For instance, the main yidam of Yeshe Tsogyal, the great yogini who was the consort of Guru Padmasambhava, was the male deity Vajrakilaya. It is also true that some great yoginis have specialized in the meditation of female deities such as Vajrayogini. In the Sakya tradition great yoginis often tend to concentrate more on the female deity Vajrayogini than on the male one, Hevajra, but again there are many exceptions to this.

The female buddha Tara, saviouress of all beings   *119*

120 Padmasambhava, 'second buddha' and master of vajrayana

Vajrayogini, principal goddess of anuttara tantra

Although buddhas may show themselves as male or female, in actual fact our buddha nature encompasses both male and female. The essence of enlightenment is non-duality. Furthermore, within all beings there are the elements of both male and female. So though the outer form of a buddha appears as either male or female, enlightenment is only achieved through reconciliation of both these aspects of our being.

12. How can it be compassionate if we just sit on our meditation cushions without doing anything? How does this help other beings?

It is not that we are doing nothing. We are training in the skilful means that will finally enable us to benefit others. One might just as well say that medical students who spend seven years in medical training before going out to operate on people are wasting their time in doing so. Of course they are not, because it is only that long training which will equip them with the means to benefit others, instead of treating people prematurely and probably causing harm. So it is with the training of dharma. We need daily meditation, periods of intense study and meditation retreats. Whether it can be said to be compassionate comes down to the motivation. As Buddha said, motivation is the most important factor in determining the value of any action. If we have the right motivation in undertaking spiritual training, then even sitting in silence or going into solitary meditation retreat are acts that will have an immensely positive outcome for others.

I must also add that those who are very accomplished in meditation are able to benefit others even when they remain in retreat. They can do this through their prayers and the extension of their benevolence to sentient beings. So we should not think that hermits or great meditators are in some way cut off from the world, whilst we are fully integrated with it. Their prayers can and do aid us even now.

13. There are many rituals in vajrayana such as prostrations, circumambulations and so on. Are they not somehow too Tibetan for us Western people?

The first thing to note here is that they are actually not Tibetan in origin but Indian. This is a very important point because there was a distinction between the culture of India and the culture of Tibet in the eighth century, just as now there is a gap between Tibet and our own culture. India was in many respects a sophisticated South Asian caste-based society and Tibet was a rather simple Central-Asian nomadic pastoralist society. There was probably nearly as much difference between those two societies as there is between any Asian society and the modern Western one.

The essential point is that Buddha's teachings go beyond culture. He prescribed all kinds of spiritual methods, including physical techniques such as prostrations and circumambulations, as ways to combat various negative tendencies that occlude our true nature. For instance, prostrations are a great remedy for pride. Do we really think Westerners are more humble than Tibetans or Indians? I doubt that very much. By prostrating we are engaging with devotion to the Three Jewels in a very unambiguous way. We are not simply paying lip service to the Three Jewels but actually developing openness and humility through our very body. Therefore, it is an effective method for developing the qualities for which we strive. Kalu Rinpoche used to say that he could see no important difference between Tibetans and Westerners. As he put it, 'The true nature of mind, the buddha nature, is the same in Tibet and the West and likewise it is covered by the same obscurations in both places.' In the light of this one

123

might well ask what is the real difference? We might have a few more computers in the West but otherwise we are not so different.

14. Why, in some Buddhist centres in the West, including yours, do people recite their prayers in Tibetan and not English?

There is no strict rule here and even in our centres, there is actually a mixture. When in groups, people generally use the Tibetan but sometimes people do their prayers in English at home. This is still a period of translation in the West and with all respect to those who are engaged in translating, I do not think that anybody would claim that we have yet arrived at definitive translations of any of the texts, whether they are the great philosophical treatises or the basic prayers that people use in their daily practice. So in order that we do not distort the meaning of these texts by arriving at a premature, incomplete or even erroneous translation, it is better to signify the provisional nature of these translations by not discarding the Tibetan.

This may sound like we are moving towards the period when all the practices will be done in English and that might well be the case. There is nothing intrinsically sacred about the Tibetan language. When Buddhism came to Tibet from India, only the mantras of vajrayana were kept in Sanskrit. The rest of the Sanskrit material was translated into Tibetan and in translating from Tibetan to English, the same approach would be applied.

15. With which lamas do we have samaya?

As we have seen earlier, samaya is the bond or commitment that is created when we take an initiation. Whichever level of tantra it may belong to, an initiation introduces us directly to the aspect of our buddha nature that is embodied in the form of the deity. From then on, there is a connection that exists between the deity, the lama who bestows that deity, and the person who receives the initiation.

There are many aspects of samaya in vajrayana but the most crucial one is the relationship with the lama. We must try from the time of initiation onwards to see him or her as inseparable from the deity. After all, it is only the extent to which he is identical to the deity that enables him to introduce us to that deity in the initiation. Even if it is a lama from whom you only take one initiation and subsequently never see again, you still have samaya with that lama from then onwards. That samaya is expressed at the end of each initiation when the disciple repeats the words, 'As the master commands, so I will do.' Everybody who has received vajrayana initiation has repeated those words since all initiations conclude in this way.

Whomever you take an initiation from is your vajra master. That means of course that you can have many vajrayana masters in your life. Obviously, one or two of them will be of the most significance to you. They are the ones from whom you take the essential guidance that affords you success on the spiritual path. This does not diminish the fact that any master from whom you have received a vajrayana initiation is your vajrayana master and you have samaya with him. Regardless of whether or not you consider them one of your principal lamas, the consequences of breaking samaya bestowed by a lama are severe. To break samaya with one's master is to turn one's back on the enlightened energy that was transmitted to one during the initiation. By doing so one alienates oneself from the spiritual path.

16. If one has received many initiations, is it necessary to practise the sadhanas of all of them?

It will not actually be possible to realize the qualities of any of the deities if one tries to practise too many of them. As it is said in Tibet, 'If you try to practise a hundred deities you will not get the benefit of one. Yet if you practise effectively just one, you will get the benefit of one hundred.' So, although we may receive an initiation, it might well be our master's advice not to rely upon that deity at that time.

One may then ask why people take many initiations. There are two answers here. The first reason is that it is beneficial to take initiations because they renew one's vows. If there have been breakages of vows or the samayas of previous initiations, these are purified by each initiation one takes. The second reason for taking initiations is that one might well need to rely on this deity at some time in the future, even if it is not appropriate now.

17. If you have taken initiations and vows with a teacher who you later discover was not qualified, are you still bound to the commitments you have made?

Sakya Pandita says that we are not bound by vows to such people because they have not been able to bestow anything genuine upon us. However, one must be careful about this. Having taken an initiation from a fully qualified lama, if one later becomes contemptuous of him, one has committed the first root downfall of vajrayana. Thus, having received initiations from a fully qualified master, it is essential that one continues to perceive him with pure vision. In this respect it is very helpful to rely upon the regular practice of guru-yoga in which one visualizes one's master as a buddha.

There are stories of great masters who sometimes behaved in ways that were absolutely contrary to normal expectations. For example, the way that some teachers like Tilopa treated their students in order to cause them to recognize the nature of their mind sometimes involved actions and instructions that might appear shocking. If a fully qualified master behaves in that way towards us, we must maintain a pure view of him and his teachings.

18. Some people take initiations without actually knowing what they have got involved in. Does this make the samaya less serious?

I am afraid that in Buddhism ignorance is not an excuse. In the 'Fourteen Downfalls of Vajrayana' Jetsun Drakpa Gyaltsen specifies ignorance as one of the four causes of breaking vows. The other three are lack of respect, lack of vigilance and being under the influence of the mental poisons. The point is that one has responsibility for a breakage even if the cause was ignorance. Perhaps one can say that it is the least meretricious of the motivations and so the consequences might be somewhat less than a breakage caused by, for example, hatred. Nevertheless, one would still have broken the sacred vows.

19. When we read the biographies of Indian and Tibetan teachers from the past, sometimes these sound rather unrealistic. How much is true and how much has been added by their students as an act of respect?

There are actually different types of biographies found in dharma. For instance, in Tibet most biographies and dharma histories were written in a very precise fashion, being concerned primarily with recording the master's training, the various teachings he or she

127

received and to whom they were transmitted. Having said that, in many of the biographies of the great Indian yogins far less attention was given to notions of historical accuracy than was given in later Tibetan texts. Furthermore, certain texts, such as the 'treasure' texts concerning Guru Padmasambhava, could be understood as being a kind of mixing together of external events and the inner landscape of spiritual experiences. On a subtle level such biographies explain how great masters dealt with the various crises that arose on the spiritual path, how these were resolved, and how spiritual power was developed. In other words, they are more concerned with spiritual events than with providing an accurate chronology of external events.

Are these true? Of course they are true, in the sense that they give us a consistent, spiritually powerful and beneficial account of the spiritual path, as displayed in the life and experience of these great masters.

20. Can meditation help people to stop taking drugs?

Meditation cannot help people to stop taking drugs. People cannot meditate *until* they stop taking drugs. Meditation can only help in the sense that if one has a sincere desire to meditate, one will remove any obstacles in one's life that prevent one from doing so, and one will therefore stop taking drugs. It is a question of whether one values a life of self-indulgence, or whether one values practising the dharma.

21. Are the experiences of taking drugs the same as the experiences of meditation?

Certain drugs, the so-called psychedelic ones, are particularly acute in the way they can trigger off experiences which may mimic meditative states. However, the person in whom these experiences arise has neither renunciation nor bodhichitta and lacks the discriminative wisdom with which to be able to utilize these experiences. Therefore, the most one can say is that they are like the dream of a spiritual experience rather than the experience itself. One must concede that occasionally what we experience in a dream motivates us to seek it in waking life. That could be why from time to time drug experiences trigger off a spiritual search in people. However, times move on and it seems more and more the case that drugs are revealing their true face, which is a destructive one. They damage not only people's spiritual capacity but, as we can often see, the fabric of society itself.

22. There are many books about tantric sex. Could you explain more about this?

Most of these books about tantric sex are just money-spinning enterprises that have nothing to do with anything spiritually or even historically authentic.

One can say that the entire vajrayana is concerned with the transmutation of sense experience into the path to enlightenment. Sense experience is not itself intrinsically impure but is made so by the impure projections of the deluded mind. In vajrayana we try to experience the underlying purity of whatever actions we engage in by using such methods as visualization of ourselves and others as deities. This pure vision is the core of the vajrayana and expresses the inseparability of samsara and nirvana.

As we have seen earlier, the meditations of anuttara tantra are divided into the development and completion stages. In the latter there are practices based upon the subtle body comprised of winds, channels and drops. Through such practices as *tummo* we strive to bring about an experience of great bliss through this subtle body. Although most of these completion stage yogas are accomplished by the yogin in solitude, there are some completion stage yogas that are to be done in conjunction with a consort. In some cases, this consort is visualized, but at other times he or she can be an actual physical person. In that case, the partner must be fully consecrated by initiation and maintain all the samaya vows. In order to be able to perform these practices, the yogin must have a considerable mastery of the other completion stage yogas. Such practices are therefore rare and are practised with a great deal of secrecy. Moreover, such practices with a consort are not permitted to monks or nuns, since they would contravene their vows of celibacy. Certainly, no genuine instructions for these types of yoga have been published in Western languages, despite the fact that there are two or three books that pretend to reveal these secret teachings.

23. *The Tibetan Book of the Dead* is very popular in the West nowadays. Do you think that Westerners who are not Buddhist should read it?

One must ask whether there is any point in them doing so because this teaching, actually called the *Bardo Thodrol*, depends on the acceptance of the doctrines of rebirth and intermediate state. This text explains how we can obtain liberation during the processes of dying and rebirth. Thus, if you do not believe that consciousness continues after death, this teaching would be merely a quaint curiosity.

Perhaps it is useful to explain a little more about this subject, since it is an important one and provokes a great deal of speculation. The word 'bardo', or intermediate state, literally means 'that which lies between'. In this case it refers to the gap which lies between the moment of death and the subsequent moment of rebirth, or more precisely conception. In the tantras, especially those of the Nyingma school, it is explained that at the moment of death one's consciousness is reunited with the ground of all awareness, sometimes known as 'the mother luminosity'. At that moment there is an opportunity to recognize our primordial nature, the dharmakaya itself. In most cases, however, due to the weight of the imprints of past actions, we fail to recognize the luminosity of reality and fall into a kind of faint.

Subsequent to the moment of death and immediately upon the consciousness being precipitated out of the body, there is a second encounter with the clear light of ultimate reality followed by a further period of unconsciousness, a kind of swoon, after which we awaken within the bardo itself. In the bardo we undergo various encounters with our primordial nature, experienced as a series of peaceful, semi-wrathful and wrathful deities, all of whom are manifestations of the basic radiance of our mind. With each of these repeated encounters, there is an opportunity for us to gain liberation by recognizing that this deity is nothing other than a projection of our own mind. Here again, the propensities of ignorance are so strong that in most cases we do not recognize them.

Thus we progress through the bardo until we reach its final stage, known as the bardo of becoming. This is like the ante-chamber of rebirth. At this point, the effects of our past karmic activity have reasserted themselves and start to shape the pattern of our future life. If at this time we can cut through the chains of karma, we can prevent rebirth into an unfortunate state and instead take a compassionate rebirth to benefit others.

131

If we cannot cut through the chains of karma in this manner, it is inevitable that we will be driven on to conception by the power of our previous actions. For most beings there is no element of personal choice here. We are simply propelled into rebirth by our imprints. The bardo comes to an end at the moment of conception when the consciousness of the being in the intermediate state fuses with the sperm and the ovum of their future parents.

Though this teaching is explained in various tantras, the most detailed account of it is found in the *Bardo Thodrol*, a collection of treasure-texts concealed by Guru Padmasambhava, which was discovered and disseminated by the treasure revealer Karma Lingpa in the fourteenth century. This is what has become popular in the West under the erroneous name of *The Tibetan Book of the Dead*. In the Nyingma tradition these teachings are given as a kind of appendix to the teachings of dzog chen. It is said that through dzog chen we can recognize the true nature of mind in this very life and therefore do not have to enter into the bardo. If we cannot achieve this level of realization during our lifetime, then the technique known as *phowa*, or consciousness transference, affords us the opportunity to achieve liberation of the moment of death through uniting one's mind with the Buddha Amitabha and obtaining rebirth in his pure realm.

However, if we have not gained mastery of phowa, we will have to rely on the teachings we have been given on the bardo. So in this sense there are three opportunities for liberation provided for us: first, during life through dzog chen teachings; secondly, at the moment of death through phowa; and thirdly, at the moment following death, through the bardo teachings.

24. Who are the revealers of the treasure-teachings and how do we know if they are genuine?

Recognizing that people in future generations will have particular specific needs and difficulties to overcome, Padmasambhava, aided by his disciples Yeshe Tsogyal and Vairochana, concealed a large number of esoteric instructions in the form of cipher manuscripts and sacred objects in various places throughout Tibet. These have been discovered at the predicted times throughout the centuries by the so-called 'treasure revealers' (tertons) who are recognized as emanations of the original 25 major disciples of Padmasambhava.

The treasure revealers, who discovered, decoded and disseminated these teachings, were blessed by Guru Padmasambhava to discover them in their former lives as his disciples. They were not ordinary people who chanced upon or made up these teachings, or archaeologists who simply translated some formerly forgotten texts.

Someone might claim to be a treasure revealer but only the treasures that have spiritual efficacy can be judged to be authentic. Padmasambhava himself acknowledged that there would be ten false treasure revealers for every genuine one. That is why in Tibet a great deal of care was always taken in assessing whether a treasure revealer was genuine. Accomplished masters would examine the teaching and only when they confirmed its authority, would it be accepted. For instance, when Chogyur Dechen Lingpa (1829–70) first revealed his treasure teachings, they were carefully checked by Situ Rinpoche of Papung before he was acknowledged to be a genuine treasure revealer.

Glossary

WAY of

Note

The majority of terms defined herein are in a phoneticized form of Sanskrit, the language of mahayana Buddhism in India. Where Tibetan terms are used, they are also in phonetics and are indicated as such by *(Tib.)* when the language is not obvious from the context.

- **Abhidharma** 'Further *dharma*'. *Buddha's* teachings on philosophy and one of the *three baskets* of the scriptures.

- **Anuttara tantra** The fourth and highest of the four tantra sets as delineated in the *new tantra schools*. Anuttara tantra is itself sub-divided into the development stage and completion stage.

- **Anu-yoga** The second of the three 'inner *tantras*' and eighth of the nine dharma vehicles distinguished in the Nyingma school.

- **Ati-yoga** The third of the triad of 'inner tantras' and ninth of the nine dharma vehicles distinguished in the Nyingma school. It comprises the teachings of dzok chen, according to which all phenomena of samsara and *nirvana* are primordially pure. Since everything is therefore perfect as it is, enlightenment can be attained without any need for acceptance or rejection.

- **Bardo** 'Intermediate state', usually between death and rebirth.

- **Bodhichitta** 'Thought of enlightenment'. Bodhichitta is characterized by the altruistic resolution to attain supreme enlightenment for the benefit of all beings and the application of this resolve in spiritual practice. Ultimate bodhichitta is insight into the fundamental emptiness of all phenomena.

• **Bodhisattva** The spiritual ideal of mahayana. A being in whom the bodhichitta has arisen and who has thus dedicated himself or herself to the achievement of enlightenment for all beings.

• **Brahma** A powerful god worshipped in early Brahmanical tradition. According to some theories he was the creator of the universe.

• **Buddha** 'Awakened One' This term may refer to the historical Buddha Shakyamuni (e.g. 'The Buddha first taught in Varanasi'), or indicate any enlightened being (e.g. 'I pray to the buddhas of the past, present and future'). In the present publication we have capitalized the 'B' in the former usage only, in order to allow the reader to distinguish easily between these two senses. In both senses, Buddha is the first of the Three Jewels.

• **Buddha nature** The innate potential for enlightenment endowed with the qualities of wisdom, compassion and power, the realization of which is complete enlightenment. *Buddha* taught that this exists within all sentient beings but is obscured by their adventitious defilements.

• **Chenrezi** *(Tib.)* The *bodhisattva* of compassion known in Sanskrit as Avalokiteshvara, a *yidam* popular in all traditions.

• **Chittamatra** One of the two major mahayana philosophical schools developed in India. It was founded by Asanga and Vasubhandu in the fourth century.

137

- **Dharma** 'The truth'. The teachings of the *Buddha* that lead one to enlightenment. The second of the Three Jewels. 'Dharmas' (plural) usually means 'phenomena' and in this sense is quite distinct from the former meaning.

- **Dzok chen** *(Tib.)* 'The Great Perfection'. See *Ati-Yoga*.

- **Four Thoughts** The preciousness of human rebirth, impermanence, cause and effect, and the sufferings of *samsara*. These are studied, reflected and meditated upon in all four of the Tibetan Buddhist traditions in order to engender renunciation, an essential quality of the *dharma* path.

- **Hinayana** 'The Small Vehicle' The hinayana comprises the foundations of the Buddhist path and is characterized by renunciation of samsara and the wish for liberation. See also *mahayana* and *vajrayana*.

- **Initiation** (abhisheka) The ritual ceremony in which the vajra master leads his student into the *mandala* or 'circle' of a tantric deity, thus conferring upon him or her the power to attain realization of that particular deity. Through initiation one enters into the vajrayana.

- **Kadam**
Influential Tibetan *dharma* tradition, founded by Dromton (1005–64), disciple of the great Atisha. Became very powerful in the 12th and 13th centuries but was in decline by the 14th century, later dying out as an independent tradition. Its teachings were preserved in the *kagyu* and gelug schools.

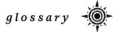

- **Kagyu**
The Kagyu tradition was founded by Marpa in the 11th century.
One of the four remaining traditions of Tibetan Buddhism.

- **Karma**
'Actions', which can be either virtuous, non-virtuous or neutral and
which are the causal basis of the states of happiness, suffering and
stillness that we experience in samsara.

- **Karma Thinley Rinpoche** Grand Master of the Dechen
Community. Born in Nangchen in Kham in 1931 and recognized
at the age of two and a half years as the *tulku* of Beru Shaiyak by
H.H. Sakya Trizin, Dakshul Thinley Rinchen. He was subsequently
recognized by the sixteenth Gyalwa Karmapa as the fourth *tulku* of
Karma Thinley. He is a master of the *Sakya* and *Kagyu* lineages of
Tibetan Buddhism.

- **Lama** *(Tib.)* In Sanskrit 'Guru'. In the Tibetan tradition a fully
qualified lama can teach the *hinayana, mahayana* and *vajrayana*.

- **Lung** *(Tib.)* 'Reading transmission'. The formal reading of a
dharma text by a teacher to a student, authorizing the latter to
study and practise the teachings contained in the text.

- **Madhyamaka** 'The Middle Way View'. The philosophical school
established by Nagarjuna (1st–2nd century AD). Its central
concern is emptiness, the realization of which sunders all clinging
to the extreme views of eternalism and nihilism.

- **Mahamudra** 'The Great Seal'. Generally in the new tantric
schools, this term denotes the realization of primordial wisdom
attained through *anuttara tantra*. In the Kagyu school, it is the

meditative accomplishment transmitted from buddha Vajradhara to the Indian siddhas Tilopa and Saraha down to the contemporary holders of the lineage through which one directly settles in and realizes the true nature of mind.

• **Mahayana** 'The Great Vehicle'. The mahayana is entered by taking the *bodhisattva* vow and its fruit is buddhahood. It is distinguished from the *hinayana* by its more profound wisdom and vaster compassion.

• **Mandala** 1. The completely pure realm of a *vajrayana* deity, whether constructed, painted or visualized. 2. A symbolic representation of the universe for the purpose of making offerings to the Three Jewels. This usually takes the form of a disc of precious metal, representing the ground, covered by piles of rice or gems, representing various marvellous features of the universe to be offered.

• **Manjushri** The bodhisattva of wisdom.

• **Mantra** Literally, 'That which protects the mind'. In *vajrayana* a mantra is principally a type of spell employed in the evocation of deities and thus serves as the pre-eminent means for accomplishing siddhis.

• **New tantra schools** *Dharma* traditions established during the second of the two diffusions of *dharma* from India to Tibet, such as the Kadam and Sakya. These new ('sarma') schools are called such in contrast to the Nyingma, or 'ancient' tradition of the first diffusion.

• **Nirvana** State of complete pacification achieved through dharma. In the *hinayana*, it is regarded as the termination of suffering for oneself. In the *mahayana* it is regarded as a temporary state that is to be transcended before arriving at buddhahood in which one returns to samsara to benefit beings. Buddhahood is therefore sometimes referred to as the 'Great Nirvana' by mahayanists in order to distinguish it from the hinayanist nirvana.

- **Nyingma** 'Ancient Ones' One of the four major Tibetan traditions which preserve the earlier transmission of *dharma* teachings which came from India to Tibet in the 8th century.

- **Prasangika** One of the divisions of madhyamaka, deriving from Buddhapalita and Chandrakirti. This system upholds the madhyamaka view by refuting all other philosophical positions about the nature of reality by exposing their absurdity. According to prasangika thinkers ultimate truth is not directly accessible to the conceptual mind. They therefore avoid making any positive assertions about ultimate reality.

- **Pratyekabuddha** 'Solitary Realizer'. A particular kind of practitioner of the *hinayana* who prefers to practise in solitude rather than amongst the *sangha*.

- **Rimé** The ecumenical or non-sectarian movement that started in the nineteenth century, inspired by Jamgön Kongtrul the Great, a Kagyu master, Chogyur Dechen Lingpa, a Nyingma master, and Jamyang Khyentse Wangpo, a Sakya master.

- **Rinpoche** 'Precious one'. An honorific title given to *tulkus* and other eminent masters.

- **Sadhana** A type of *vajrayana* ritual text, as well as the actual meditation practice it sets out.

- **Sakya Trizin** The head of the Sakya tradition. The current Sakya Trizin is Ngawang Kunga Thegchen Palbar, born 1945 in Tsedong, south western Tibet.

- **Samaya** 'Sacred Commitment'. The vows and pledges taken during a *vajrayana* initiation, the most important of which is the pledge to always see the guru as inseparable from the *yidam* of the initiation.

- **Samsara** The endless cycle of birth and death among the six realms of hell, ghosts, animals, humans, demigods and gods, all of which are flawed by subtle or gross forms of suffering. One is reborn in these through the process of *karma.*

- **Shravaka** 'Hearer'. A particular kind of practitioner of *hinayana* who prefers to practise amongst the sangha rather than in solitude.

- **Siddha** 'Accomplished one'. A tantric practitioner who has attained *siddhis* and possesses mastery over the phenomenal world as a result of his enlightened insight into its fundamental purity.

- **Siddhi** 'Accomplishment', which comes about from *vajrayana* practice. There are two kinds: enlightenment itself and worldly siddhis such as health, wealth and intelligence, which help one on the path towards enlightenment.

- **Sutra** 'Discourse'. One of the *three baskets* taught by the *Buddha*. Sutras are generally said to contain teachings on meditation, whereas the others two 'baskets', *vinaya* and *abhidharma,* teach moral conduct and philosophy respectively. However, this is a generalization since there are elements of all three categories of teaching in the sutras. The term is sometimes used in contrast to *tantra* to refer to all the non-tantric teachings of the *Buddha*.

• **Svatantrika** The division of madhyamaka founded by Bhavaviveka. Through syllogistic reasoning this system refutes the notion that phenomena have intrinsic nature and then establishes that their true nature is emptiness.

• **Svatantrika Madhyamaka Yogachara** A philosophical and meditative system that combines *svatantrika* madhyamaka with yogachara first brought to Tibet by Shantarakshita.

• **Tantra** The tantras are the scriptural sources of *vajrayana* Buddhism.

• **Tara** *A vajrayana yidam.* She has several different forms, perhaps the most popular of which is green Tara who is the embodiment of Buddha activity.

• **Three baskets** *Sutra, abhidharma* and *vinaya.* These comprise the non-tantric teachings of the *Buddha.* They were preserved in an oral tradition amongst *Buddha's* followers before being written down many generations later.

• **Three jewels** *Buddha, dharma* and sangha, the principle sources of refuge. One becomes a Buddhist by taking refuge in these.

• **Three vehicles** *Hinayana, mahayana* and *vajrayana.* These may be said to comprise three increasingly subtle and powerful methods of practising the dharma path. Strictly however, *vajrayana* is a sub-division of *mahayana*, which can be divided into 'ordinary' (non-tantric) and 'extraordinary' (tantric, i.e. *vajrayana*).

- **Tulku** *(Tib.)* A reincarnate *lama.* The system of recognizing the rebirths of great lamas was initially developed in Tibet by the *Karma Kagyu* tradition.

- **Vajrakilaya** A wrathful *yidam* from the maha yoga of the *Nyingma* tradition, said to be especially powerful in degenerate times, such as these.

- **Vajrayana** Literally, 'The Indestructible Vehicle'. The vajrayana is a special part of the *mahayana.* Taught by *Buddha* in the *tantras,* it provides the most powerful instructions for fulfilling the *bodhisattva* vow and so achieving enlightenment.

- **Vajrayogini** One of the principal *yidams* of the Sakya tradition.

- **Vedas** The earliest Brahmanical scriptures comprised of four main cycles and believed in the Indian tradition to have been revealed by sages at the beginning of this world era.

- **Vinaya** The *Buddha's* teachings on moral conduct and one of the *three baskets.* These teachings are the source of monastic vows.

- **Yidam** *(Tib.)* Literally, 'That to which one's mind is committed'. A yidam is a manifestation of the enlightened mind of the *buddhas* in the form of a deity. Having received a *vajrayana* initiation of a certain yidam, one maintains *samaya* vows and practises the *sadhana* of the *yidam* in order to attain *siddhis.*

- **Yoga** Literally, 'union'. In Tibetan works this term usually refers to various vajrayana meditation practices.

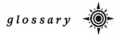
- **Yogin** Male practitioner of *yoga*.

- **Yogini** Female practitioner of *yoga*.

About the Author

Jampa Thaye (Dr David Stott) is a meditation master and scholar of the Sakya and Kagyu traditions of Buddhism. For the past three decades he has studied under Karma Thinley Rinpoche and H.H. Sakya Trizin as well as various other masters of Vajrayana. As Karma Thinley Rinpoche's dharma regent he directs the Dechen Community in Europe and has authored a number of books. Jampa Thaye has a doctorate in Tibetan religious history and has lectured for many years at both Manchester Metropolitan University and the University of Manchester.